THE DOCTRINE OF CONSIDERATION.

T0371043

THE HISTORY OF

THE DOCTRINE OF CONSIDERATION

IN ENGLISH LAW.

(BEING THE YORKE PRIZE ESSAY FOR THE YEAR 1891)

BY

EDWARD JENKS, M.A.,

OF THE MIDDLE TEMPLE, BARRISTER-AT-LAW;
FELLOW OF KING'S COLLEGE, CAMBRIDGE;
PROFESSOR OF LAW IN UNIVERSITY COLLEGE, LIVERPOOL.

LONDON:
C. J. CLAY AND SONS,
CAMBRIDGE UNIVERSITY PRESS WAREHOUSE,
AVE MARIA LANE.

1892

[*All Rights reserved.*]

CAMBRIDGE
UNIVERSITY PRESS

University Printing House, Cambridge CB2 8BS, United Kingdom

Cambridge University Press is part of the University of Cambridge.

It furthers the University's mission by disseminating knowledge in the pursuit of education, learning and research at the highest international levels of excellence.

www.cambridge.org
Information on this title: www.cambridge.org/9781316626214

© Cambridge University Press 1892

This publication is in copyright. Subject to statutory exception and to the provisions of relevant collective licensing agreements, no reproduction of any part may take place without the written permission of Cambridge University Press.

First published 1892
First paperback edition 2016

A catalogue record for this publication is available from the British Library

ISBN 978-1-316-62621-4 Paperback

Cambridge University Press has no responsibility for the persistence or accuracy of URLs for external or third-party internet websites referred to in this publication, and does not guarantee that any content on such websites is, or will remain, accurate or appropriate.

TO

THE HON. GEORGE HIGINBOTHAM,
CHIEF JUSTICE OF VICTORIA.

Dear Mr Chief Justice,

to your kindness I owe the permission accorded me to make use of the valuable library of the Supreme Court in Melbourne. It seems meet therefore, to dedicate to you the following pages, which, but for that permission, I could not have produced. If it were not that the imperfection of my work might detract from the value of my admiration, I should like to add that I know of no one more worthily deserving, on public and private grounds alike, of the esteem and respect of those who, like myself, love the study no less than the practice of the law. Now that I have left the great colony of which you are, next to Her Majesty's direct representative, the official head, I trust that I shall be accused neither of presumption nor of sycophancy if I sign myself,

Your affectionate and admiring friend,

EDWARD JENKS.

PREFACE.

THE following pages were written in Melbourne, where the writer had not the opportunity of seeing Professor Ames' valuable articles on the History of Assumpsit, which appeared in the *Harvard Law Review* for the months of April and May 1888. The references to those articles have since been added, with the permission of the authorities. The writer's indebtedness to Mr Justice Holmes' work on *The Common Law* will probably be manifest to any one who takes the trouble to read his essay; but he would deem himself wanting in gratitude did he not here make a formal and personal acknowledgment of it. The only other thing which it seems necessary to say is, that the rules of the University on the subject of the Yorke Prize compel the publication of the successful essay in a permanent form.

Library of the Middle Temple,
September, 1892.

CONTENTS.

CHAPTER I.

CHAPTER II.

CHAPTER III.

CHAPTER IV.

CHAPTER I.

THE DOCTRINE OF CONSIDERATION AT THE PRESENT DAY.

AT the present day, the doctrine of Consideration plays a part in the law relating to two great juristic institutions, Contracts and Conveyances. Whatever may have been the relationship between these institutions in former times, whether the one grew out of the other, or whether both are original conceptions of juristic activity, it is certain that all modern systems recognise a clear distinction between them. Both are arrangements entered into between individuals or corporations with the view of affecting their legal relationships. Both are recognised and, in most cases, actively enforced by judicial tribunals. But the contract is prospective in its character, it creates new duties and rights; while the conveyance operates fully at once, merely transferring existing duties or rights[1]. Every con-

[1] The writer is aware of the objections which have been raised to the expression " transfer of a right." Perhaps it is strictly true that a right cannot be transferred. But the substitution of a precisely similar relationship between A and C for that previously existing between A and B, resembles a transfer so closely as to warrant the expression.

tract contains a promise: many contracts contain several[1]. A conveyance, on the other hand, is complete, and leaves nothing to be done on either side. It is true that a conveyance may have contracts attached to it, either implied by law or expressed in documentary form. But, for all that, the conveyance and the contract are clearly separable in idea; and give rise to different branches of legal learning. We will begin with the subject of contract, for, at the present day, the Doctrine of Consideration is much more important in the Law of Contract than in the Law of Conveyance.

A.

The present Doctrine of Consideration as it relates to Contract is to be gathered from Acts of Parliament and judicial decisions. These are, strictly speaking, the only authoritative expositors of the doctrine, although it is possible that one or two of its canons, handed down by tradition, and so universally adopted that they have never been called in question, have not yet received express sanction. But the doctrine has also been the subject of careful attention among modern text-book writers, and it may be worth while, as a preliminary exercise, to state the conclusions at which they have arrived. We can afterwards test these conclusions by reference to authority.

---

[1] "Where performance on both sides is simultaneous, there may be agreement in the wider sense, but there is no obligation and no contract." Pollock, *Principles of Contract*, 5th edition, p. 166.

It is believed that the following canons represent, in a compact form, the opinions of modern English writers.

1. *Every true contract contains a promise. A consideration is a detriment voluntarily incurred by the promisee [or a benefit conferred on the promisor at the instance of the promisee] in exchange for the promise.*

This, it is submitted, is the general sense of the text-books on the subject, though some of them express themselves obscurely. It may be taken as the view of Smith[1] and Anson[2]. Addison does not furnish a definition, and Leake[3] is very vague. Chitty is positively misleading when he speaks of "a sufficient consideration or recompense for making, *or motive or inducement to make,* the promise upon which a party is charged[4]." The clause within the brackets has been questioned in deference to the opinion of Pollock, who seems[5] to doubt its authority. But, apart from judicial precedent, upon which the full canon is based, it seems impossible to say that, when A promises to give X a horse if he will abstain from obstructing his (A's) admission to a syndicate or club, and X abstains, without the smallest trouble or inconvenience to

[1] *The Law of Contracts,* 5th ed. p. 154.

[2] *Principles of the English Law of Contracts,* 4th ed. p. 68.

[3] "Some matter accepted or agreed for, as a return for the promise made." *Digest of the Law of Contracts,* 1st ed. p. 17.

[4] *Treatise on the Law of Contracts,* 12th ed. p. 19.

[5] *Principles of Contract,* p. 166.

himself[1], this will not be a consideration to support *A*'s promise[2].

2. *Such consideration may be either the performance or the promise of an act or forbearance. If it be the performance, the consideration is said to be* **executed;** *if the promise, to be* **executory**.

This is the language of the most modern writers, such as Pollock[3], Anson[4], and Leake[5]. Pollock puts it thus—" A consideration which is itself a promise is said to be *executory*. A consideration which consists in performance is said to be *executed*[3]." Unfortunately, the writers of a slightly earlier date confound *executed* consideration with *past* consideration. Smith and Chitty are clearly guilty of this charge. The former says[6]—" An executed consideration is one which has already taken place, an executory consideration one which is to take place, one is past, the other future. Thus, if *A* delivered goods to *B* yesterday, and *B* makes a promise to-day in consideration of that delivery, this promise is said to be founded upon an executed consideration, because the delivery of the goods is past and over." To the same effect Chitty, who draws elaborate distinctions between considerations " executed," " executory," " concurrent " and " continuing," without finding any place for the ordinary instance of the

---

[1] e.g. by simply refraining from handing in a black ball.

[2] "The ordinary rule is, that any act done whereby the contracting party receives a benefit is a good consideration for a promise by him." Martin, B. in *Scotson v. Pegg*, 6 H. and N. at p. 299.

[3] p. 166.   [4] p. 89.   [5] p. 18.   [6] p. 179.

giving of an act for a promise[1]. In like manner some writers have drawn a distinction between executory and executed *contracts*, apparently confounding "executory" with "unilateral[2]." There can be little doubt of the superiority of the most recent phraseology, which treats past consideration as no consideration[3], reduces all true considerations to the two classes of performance and promise, and calls nothing a contract unless it is executory—i.e. unless something remains to be done in performance of it[4].

With regard to executory considerations, however, care is necessary if we would avoid confusion. Inasmuch as the consideration is itself a promise, it follows that, if the contract be formless, there must be a consideration for it also[5]. This consideration is, of course, the counter-promise of the promisor, so that the element which is in one aspect a consideration, is in the other a promise, and *vice versâ*. If there is an executory consideration, there will be two promises and two considerations. It is usual to speak of the party from whom the offer came as the promisee; but the acceptor is, in truth, equally in that position. The difficulty does not arise in the case of an executed consideration.

3. *The existence of a consideration is essential to the validity of every "simple" or formless contract, i.e. every contract not contained in sealed writing nor apparent on the records of a Court of Justice.*

[1] pp. 45—49. [2] Addison, p. 62.
[3] Anson, p. 92. [4] Pollock, p. 166.
[5] See 3rd Canon, *post*.

This canon is unanimously accepted by the modern writers. Anson[1], Chitty[2], Leake[3], and Smith[4] expressly enunciate it: Addison[5] and Pollock[6] allow it by clear implication. We need not waste time, therefore, by insisting upon it.

It may be well, however, to point out that a simple contract here includes the release of any former simple[7] contract, by writing not under seal, by words, or by implication[8]. This application of the canon is sometimes treated as though it were a distinct rule, and is even made the subject of unfavourable comment[9]. But it would seem that a release is really a new contract, and therefore, if not under seal or by record, requiring, on general principles, a new consideration. *A* fails to pay *X* for goods supplied, in breach of his promise. *X* releases him from his liability. What is this but a contract by *X* not to enforce his rights? And so, it requires a consideration on general principles. It is conceived that the rule would be the same, if the release were given before the payment had become due, i.e. before there was a breach of the old contract. But that is because the consideration of the old contract is *executed*. If it were still executory, mutual releases would operate as consideration for each

---

[1] p. 68.   [2] pp. 9, 19.

[3] p. 17. This writer seems, by his language, to extend the requirement to *all* contracts. (Qu. *per incuriam*.)

[4] p. 146.   [5] p. 2.   [6] p. 182.

[7] A contract under seal can only be released at law by sealed writing, which does not need a consideration. Chitty, p. 767.

[8] Chitty, p. 768.   [9] Pollock, p. 179.

other, and no other consideration would be necessary[1]. To the general rule, however, there exists a special exception in the case of negotiable instruments, which may be discharged at any time by parol without consideration[2].

A rather important corollary is deduced from the principal canon that every simple contract requires a consideration. It may be stated thus:

COROLLARY. *Where by any rule of law an agreement must be reduced to writing as a condition precedent to becoming a contract, the consideration must appear in the writing, if in fact it was stated in the agreement.*

The difficulty with regard to this corollary lies in the wording of it. In the above attempt there has been strict adherence to the definition of a contract as an executory agreement enforceable by an action at law. This course, it is submitted, overcomes the difficulty which arises on the wording of the 4th section of the Statute of Frauds[3], and which some writers have taken to imply the possibility of the existence of unenforceable contracts[4]. It is to be observed that the section only once uses the word "contract," and that in a sense which strongly leads the reader to suspect that the framer was thinking of conveyance rather than contract in the modern sense[5]. On all other occasions the

---

[1] Leake, p. 788. Chitty, p. 769.
[2] Chitty, p. 769. Byles, 14th ed. p. 266.
[3] 29 Car. II. c. 3. [4] e.g. Anson, p. 62. Smith, p. 127.
[5] *Non obstante* the modern view, which is not authoritative for literary purposes.

words used are "agreement" or "promise," and the
whole tenor of the section is to say that these
"agreements" or "promises" shall not become contracts until certain formalities are added. It may
be that they may avail for certain purposes, such
as defences to actions for money had and received:
but they will not be *enforceable by action*. This
view is entirely in harmony with the wording of the
17th section, which evidently contemplates an attempted conveyance without corporal transfer, in
accordance with the old-established notion that the
property in specific chattels passes by agreement of
the price without payment or delivery[1]. The 17th
section provides that such a conveyance (called a
"contract") shall not be allowed to be good, in the
case of sales in which the purchase money exceeds
£10. That this view of the section is not fanciful, is
proved by the long exegetical struggle which resulted
in the passing of Lord Tenterden's Act[2], a statute
professedly in this respect declaratory, but really
enacting.

With the main proposition of the corollary, all
the text-books agree[3]. But the necessity for the
final clause is not noticed by all of them. Its introduction into the doctrine of the text-books is, probably,
due to Benjamin[4]. It has been followed by Pollock[5]

[1] See Anson, p. 65, and Benjamin, *The Sale of Personal Property*, 4th ed. Book II. *passim*.

[2] 9 Geo. IV. c. 14, s. 7.

[3] Chitty, pp. 115, 116. Pollock, p. 160. Smith, p. 78. Anson,
p. 57. Leake, p. 267.

[4] p. 225.

[5] p. 160. This writer appears to hold that it is in no case

and Anson[1], the latter, however, alleging a doubtful reason for it. The true reason seems to be that an "agreement" implies an actual statement of terms, and that a term implied by law is rather in the nature of a legal rule of interpretation than a matter agreed upon by the parties. The great objection, however, to this limitation of the corollary is that its application leads to the very result which it was the avowed object of the statute to avoid. In order to shew that the consideration need not appear in the writing, it is necessary to prove the actual circumstances and details of the agreement, thereby opening the door to those very "Frauds and Perjuries" which the statute aimed at preventing.

It should be noticed also that there are two substantial exceptions to the rule laid down by the corollary. These are the cases of negotiable instruments and guarantees. In neither need the consideration appear in the writing, though the contracts themselves cannot be made by word of mouth[2].

4. *In certain cases a consideration is essential also to the validity of a contract under seal, and in nearly all cases it is a condition precedent to the granting of the special remedy of "specific performance."*

necessary to state the consideration in writing when the case falls under the 17th section of the Statute of Frauds (as amended by Tenterden's Act). But does he mean to lay it down that, if the price is expressly agreed on, it need not be stated in the writing?

[1] p. 65.

[2] Pollock, p. 160. Anson, p. 57. Smith, pp. 102, 166. Chitty, pp. 20, 596. Addison, p. 851. Leake, pp. 247, 607.

The first part of this canon applies, it is believed, only to contracts in restraint of trade, i.e. contracts by which a man binds himself not to exercise a calling within certain limits, or for a specified time. In many cases these contracts are pronounced altogether void, on the ground of "unreasonableness." And, even when they are admittedly reasonable, there must be a consideration to support them[1]. It is said also, by a text-book writer[2], that covenants to stand seised to uses are on the same footing as contracts in restraints of trade. But covenants to stand seised have, since the passing of the Statute of Uses, practically become conveyances, and will fall naturally under that division of the chapter which deals with conveyances.

The latter part of the canon is now generally received[3], the principal exceptions to the general rule occurring in the cases of family arrangements and settlements in favour of volunteers. Even here the exceptions are doubtful, and it seems that the latter class of cases includes only those in which volunteers claim the enforcement of an arrangement which is at least partly founded on consideration[4].

5. *But, in the cases contemplated by Canon 4, the consideration need not be stated in the deed.*

---

[1] Smith, p. 16. Chitty, p. 679. Pollock, p. 342. Leake, p. 737. Anson, pp. 49, 188.

[2] Smith, p. 16.

[3] Leake, pp. 147, 609, 1150. Chitty, p. 838. Anson, p. 50. Addison, p. 378. Fry, *The Specific Performance of Contracts*, 2nd ed. p. 42. May, *Voluntary Dispositions of Property*, 2nd ed. p. 390.

[4] May, p. 261. Fry, pp. 43, 363, 364.

This doctrine is only what might have been expected as result of the rule that consideration is usually demanded in a contract under seal only for the purpose of obtaining an equitable remedy. Never having been bound, until its fusion with the Courts of Law, by the strict legal rules on the subject of evidence, the Court of Chancery quite naturally deemed the mere statement of the consideration unessential. Accordingly, it is the settled rule, that a plaintiff seeking specific performance may shew any consideration not inconsistent with the terms of the deed[1].

6. *In accordance with the general rule of law, the onus of proving the existence of a consideration usually rests upon the party setting up the contract, whether the consideration appears in writing or not. But, in the case of negotiable instruments, the existence of consideration is presumed, in the absence of suspicious circumstances.*

The first part of this canon is so obvious, that several of the text-book writers do not deem it necessary to state it. But it is clearly to be gathered from their expressions. "They (bills of exchange and promissory notes) differ from other simple contracts in this—that whereas, in general, it must appear affirmatively that there was a consideration for such contracts[2]" etc. And to the same effect other writers[3]. With regard to the

---

[1] Pollock, p. 184. Leake, p. 607. Fry, p. 352. May, pp. 219, 266, 267.

[2] Chitty, p. 20.   [3] e.g. Smith, p. 166.

latter half of the rule, the text-books are clear[1], and for very obvious reasons. The bill of exchange, the original negotiable instrument, always implied that the drawer had received its value from the payee, and merely used the acceptor as his banker[2]. A contrary inference would almost have amounted to a presumption of fraud. Promissory notes were by statute early put upon the same footing as bills of exchange, and naturally adopted their rules of evidence. The fact that negotiable instruments have since come to be largely used for fictitious purposes, has not altered the rule. It should be noticed, however, that if a negotiable instrument be once proved to have been tainted with fraud[3], the presumption in favour of the existence of consideration vanishes.

7. *In ordinary cases, it is immaterial whether or no the consideration be economically adequate to the promise.*

In this doctrine the text-book writers fully agree. "The inadequacy of the consideration, in point of value, as equivalent for the promise, is immaterial in English law[4]." And to the same effect all the other standard authors[5], the reason alleged being, that the law, while it undertakes to enforce agreements in certain cases, does not undertake to make them. We need not, therefore, dwell on the rule,

[1] Chitty, p. 20. Anson, pp. 70, 76. Leake, pp. 607, 608. Addison, p. 971. Smith, p. 166. Byles, p. 3.

[2] *Non obstantibus* the expressions of Mr Justice Wilmot in *Pillans v. Van Mierop*, 3 Burr. 1673.

[3] Byles, pp. 137, 138.   [4] Leake, p. 613.

[5] Chitty, p. 22. Pollock, p. 171. Anson, pp. 69, 70. Smith, pp. 160, 207. Addison, p. 12.

merely remarking that the long discussion of cases which usually follows its statement in the text-books seems more properly to belong to another branch of the subject, viz. the *genuineness* of the consideration. Perhaps the most conclusive proof of the soundness of the canon is the fact that the value of the consideration is never regarded as fixing the amount of damages for breach of the contract.

8. *But gross inadequacy of consideration, though in itself no objection to the validity of a contract, either at law or in equity, may be evidence of fraud.*

This seems to be the greatest effect, at the present day, of inadequacy of consideration. There was formerly a tradition that inadequacy of consideration was itself a bar to the grant of specific performance, but the most recent writers are of opinion that the authorities do not warrant this view[1].

9. *On the other hand, the consideration must be genuine.*

Here is in fact the greatest difficulty in the whole doctrine. As Anson observes, "at first sight this looks like saying that a consideration must be a consideration[2]." And such is really the case, but it does not help us much. We must examine some of the favourite examples of unreal considerations put forward to support contracts, and we shall then, by a process of exclusion, arrive at some notion of what is a genuine consideration. This result will naturally

[1] Smith, p. 161. Chitty, p. 23. Leake, p. 614. Anson, p. 72. Pollock, pp. 174 and 595 (where the point is carefully discussed).
[2] p. 72.

throw some light on the definition of consideration. (See Canon 1.)

One of the oldest *dicta* on the point is, that when the consideration apparently confers a benefit on the promisor, but the benefit is only apparent, the consideration will not be held to be genuine. Thus, for example, a promise to surrender, or, it would seem, the actual surrender, of a tenancy at will, to the promisor, is no consideration, because a tenancy at will can be put an end to by either party at any time[1]. Presumably, however, a promise to surrender a tenancy at will, over which the promisee had no control, would be a consideration.

So also, a promise or the performance of an act, which the party making or rendering it is legally bound to perform, is no consideration. "If, for example, a debtor, being bound by law to give up the title-deeds of an estate to a purchaser, pursuant to a decree of sale, enters into an agreement with the purchaser, to deliver them to him on payment of a sum of money, the debtor is not only without any right of action for enforcing such an agreement, but, if the money is paid, he is himself subject to an action for the recovery of it back[2]." But here a caution is necessary. For if the promise or performance be of an act that the party making or rendering it was legally bound, not to the promisor, but to a stranger, to do, it seems the better opinion that this is a consideration, on the ground that

[1] Chitty, pp. 26, 34.
[2] Addison, p. 4, paraphrasing Pothier, p. 25.   Anson, p. 82.

the party thereby deprives himself of the power of agreeing with the stranger for a release[1].

Again, it used to be said that a so-called " moral obligation," was, in certain recognised cases, sufficient to support a promise. One particular class of such obligations was denominated " good considerations." These consisted chiefly of supposed duties towards relatives, and were perhaps originally due to the distinction made by the Roman Law between gifts to relatives and gifts to strangers. But it seems now beyond question that a moral obligation will not serve as a consideration[2].

Lastly, it may, perhaps, be accepted as the latest doctrine, that a *past* consideration, i.e. a promise or act which was made or done, not in exchange for the promise which is sought to be enforced, but prior to and independently of such promise, will not be deemed a genuine consideration[3]. Thus, if *A* has, merely as a matter of charity or friendship, given valuable assistance to *B*, and *B* afterwards, out of gratitude, promises to give *A* a sum of money in return therefor, *B*'s promise is not enforceable, as

---

[1] Pollock, p. 177. Chitty, p. 40. Leake, p. 622. See discussion of this case *post*, p. 57.

[2] Leake, p. 616. Chitty, pp. 35, 36. Pollock, p. 169. Smith, p. 188. Anson, p. 102. Addison, p. 10.

[3] Anson, p. 92. "A past consideration is, in effect, no consideration at all." Addison, p. 5. Pollock, p. 169. Chitty, p. 45 (where an executed and a past consideration are treated as identical). Leake, pp. 19, 613. Smith, p. 179, also confusing executed and past consideration. It seems usual to mix up "past" and "moral" considerations, apparently without good cause or satisfactory result.

being made without consideration. The point is, that the assistance which is relied upon was not given *in exchange for* the promise. It is, of course, unnecessary to point out that a *past* consideration differs from an *executed* consideration in this very point, viz. that it is not given, as the latter is, for the promise. *A* offers to give a reward to the person who will bring back his horse which has strayed. *B* brings back the horse, and thereby, gives an act, as executed consideration, for the promise.

Unfortunately, however, though the general rule is against the genuineness of past considerations, there are still some exceptions, occasionally unquestionable, more often doubtful.

It is for example, unquestionable, that a promise in writing[1] to pay a debt barred by the Statute of Limitations is valid without consideration[2]. Similar rules formerly prevailed with regard to debts incurred by infants, and liabilities incurred prior to a discharge in bankruptcy[3]. But these are now abolished by statute[4]. It is sometimes attempted to treat these exceptions as waivers of procedural rules imposed for the benefit of the promisor[5]. But the whole doctrine of consideration may in a sense be

---

[1] 9 Geo. IV. c. 14.

[2] Pollock, p. 170. Chitty, p. 796. Anson, p. 100. Leake, p. 991 (implied).

[3] Leake, pp. 543, 618. Anson, p. 100. Chitty, p. 206. Pollock, p. 61. Addison, p. 120.

[4] 37 and 38 Vic. c. 62. 12 and 13 Vic. c. 106, and subsequent statutes.

[5] Chitty, p. 796. Anson, p. 101. Pollock, p. 170.

said to be a procedural rule; and it is better to treat the revival of barred debts as a real exception.

More doubtful are the cases in which it is alleged that a past consideration, if moved by a previous request of the promisor, will support the promise. This is the penultimate rather than the ultimate doctrine of the text-books. It is asserted boldly by Chitty[1]—"But where the plaintiff's act is moved or procured by the request of the party who makes the promise, it will bind; for though the promise follows, yet it is not naked, but couples itself with the precedent request and the merits of the party procured by that suit." And again Addison—"Bygone acts or services will maintain an action when performed or rendered pursuant to the previous request of the promisor[2]." To the same effect Smith[3]. Leake[4] and Pollock[5], however, state the rule with great caution, and it is, practically, denied by Anson[6].

Still more doubtful are the cases in which it is alleged that a request founding a past consideration is *implied*. This allegation is made with respect to three classes of examples, and it may be as well to state each separately, for the topic as usually discussed in the books is somewhat confusing. The cases in which it is said that the act of the plaintiff is moved by an implied request of the defendant occur where—

(i) *The plaintiff has been compelled to do what*

[1] p. 46. [2] p. 9. [3] p. 179.
[4] p. 52. [5] p. 169. [6] pp. 94—97.

the defendant was legally compellable to do, but has not done[1].

This is the case of the surety who has been compelled to pay the debt of the principal debtor, because the latter has failed to do so, and who now sues the principal debtor for reimbursement; or the case of the agent who imports goods for a principal and pays import duty upon them; or of the indorser of a bill, who, on failure of the acceptor, satisfies the holder.   Not only is there no presumption in fact of the request, but it is conceived that even the direction of the defendant that the plaintiff should not perform the defendant's duty would not exonerate the latter from recouping the former if he declined to comply with the direction.   If this be the case, it would seem better to class such a liability as arising *ex lege immediate,* or *ex statu,* rather than as the result of an implied contract founded on a consideration itself based on an imaginary request.   For it should be noticed that, in this class of cases, the promise as well as the previous request may be implied[2].

(ii) *The defendant has adopted and taken advantage of the plaintiff's previous act*[3].

Here again the request and the promise are both implied.   But, in the cases which fall under this head, there is a much simpler explanation than the elaborate theory of a double implication.   It is much

[1] Smith, p. 177. Chitty, p. 47. Leake, p. 77.

[2] Smith, p. 183.

[3] Addison, p. 10. Leake, p. 78. Chitty, p. 47. Smith, p. 184.

better to say, as Anson suggests[1], that the plaintiff's act was really the offer of an executed consideration in return for a reasonable remuneration. *Id certum est quod certum reddi potest.* In this way the subsequent promise is looked upon merely as evidence fixing the measure of damages.

(iii) *The plaintiff has voluntarily done what the defendant was compellable to do, and the defendant has subsequently promised to reimburse him.*

This rule is stated with apparent confidence by some of the text-books[2], but the most modern writers have shewn good reason for refusing unqualified assent to it. The alleged authorities are very carefully examined by Anson[3], who comes to the conclusion that "it may not be safe to say that the rule as habitually laid down is non-existent, but the cases cited in support of it seem to fail, on examination, to bear it out."

On the other hand there are some instances of apparently unreal consideration which turn out to be genuine.

One of the most striking of these is the so-called deposit on trust. *B* requests *A* to allow him to perform a certain act which necessitates the deposit with him (*B*) of goods belonging to *A*. *B* either expressly or impliedly promises to return the goods to *A*, with or without remuneration for the use of them. For some time it has been undoubted law that *A* can sue *B* for non-fulfilment of his promise,

[1] p. 97.   [2] Chitty, p. 47.   Smith, p. 185.   Addison, p. 10.
[3] p. 99.

express or implied; but the nature of the action has been variously stated. Sometimes B is treated as a trustee, and the remedy of A as for breach of trust. Again, A is regarded simply as using the possessory remedy of Detinue, or the modern substitute therefor. But when there is a promise to remunerate A beyond the mere return of the goods, the matter is usually discussed on the ground of the benefit obtained by B, as an illustration of the rule that the law will not weigh the adequacy of the consideration[1].

It seems however, unnecessary to resort to this rather strained construction of the rule on the subject of adequacy. All modern definitions of consideration include the idea of detriment to the promisee, as well as of benefit to the promisor. Indeed, as we have seen[2], one writer inclines to regard the former as the only essential idea. And it seems fairly clear that the man who parts with the immediate control over goods does undergo a detriment in the risk which he incurs in the process. According to all legal ideas of value, a *chose* in possession is, other things being equal, worth more than the same *chose* in action; and the difference between the two values is the measure of the promisee's detriment. The matter is of some importance in view of the questions raised by the existence of a gratuitous agency[3].

---

[1] e.g. in Chitty (11th ed.) at p. 29 et seq.

[2] ante p. 3.

[3] In a subsequent chapter the writer has made a suggestion as to the origin of this class of cases.

A second example, of consideration apparently unreal but legally genuine, is said to occur where A, being under a liability to B, gives C a right to enforce *the same* liability, and thereupon receives a promise. "Liability to a new party in respect of a debt or obligation already incurred to another may form a sufficient consideration to support a promise by the new creditor[1]." This doctrine appears to proceed originally upon the relative character of an obligation, as a thing not existing *per se*, i.e. independently of persons of inherence, but as only imaginable in connection with distinct parties. In this view, each new party introduced into the transaction creates at least one new obligation, the undertaking of which is sufficient consideration for a promise by the obligor. It is, of course, no objection to this view that the satisfaction of one obligation, in the case put, will discharge the others. Obligations are frequently discharged otherwise than by performance. But the rule is a little hard to reconcile with (for example) the Roman doctrine of correality. It may, however, be defended on the practical ground suggested by Anson[2], and approved by Pollock[3], that the addition of a new creditor frequently prevents the debtor compounding with the original obligee.

A third and somewhat difficult class of cases occurs in connection with the settlement of disputed

---

[1] Leake, p. 626. See also Addison, p. 4. Chitty, p. 40. Anson (p. 87) and Pollock (p. 177) *dubitantibus*.

[2] p. 88.   [3] p. 178.

claims. Every lawyer would admit that the abandonment of a supportable claim to a share in an
estate, or of an undoubted right under a contract,
would constitute a genuine consideration, as a
detriment undergone by the promisee. But, suppose
the claim unfounded. Suppose the promisee mistaken in thinking himself to have a right. Is the
consideration genuine?

It would appear that if the claim abandoned
were manifestly bad in point of law, the abandonment
would not form a sufficient consideration, even
though the parties believed it to be valid[1]. Similarly,
if, in point of fact, the promisee knew that there
was no foundation for his claim[2]. But where the
promisee honestly believes himself to be abandoning
an enforceable claim, and the claim is not manifestly
bad in law, a promise given by the opposing party in
exchange for his withdrawal will be supported, even
though the claim turns out to be really baseless[3].
And it makes no difference that the *promisor* was
convinced of the unsoundness of the claim. He has
been saved the vexation and expense of litigation,
and, as the plaintiff has acted *bonâ fide*, the law,
which leans strongly in favour of compromises where
there is no public advantage to be gained by investigation, will enforce the promise.

These examples, though by no means exhaustive,

[1] Chitty, p. 27.   Leake, p. 625.

[2] Anson, p. 75.   Chitty, p. 27.

[3] Leake, p. 627.   Chitty, p. 27.   Anson, p. 75.   Addison, p.
11.   Pollock, p. 181.

will serve to illustrate the doctrine of the genuineness of consideration. We now pass to another canon.

10. *If* **executed**, *the consideration must not be an illegal or immoral act, nor, if* **executory**, *must it contemplate an illegal or immoral object.*

It seems impossible to frame this canon more exactly, owing to the fact that there is no uniform rule as to the effects of illegality or immorality in a consideration. But, before proceeding to treat of the consequences of an illegal or immoral consideration, we may allude to an initial ambiguity.

What is the difference between "illegality" and "immorality," used in this connection?

It seems clear that the term "illegality" is confined to distinct breaches of the law, which can be visited by positive punishment. A consideration which consists in the agreed abandonment of a prosecution for felonious forgery is bad, because the compounding of a felony is a definite offence, recognised and punishable by the law. But a consideration which consists in the cohabitation of unmarried persons is merely immoral, for such cohabitation is not directly punishable by law. Needless to say, that acts and intentions which are immoral in the broader sense of the term, are not in all cases immoral for the purposes of this canon. In this doctrine the law treats as immoral only irregular sexual connections, the limitation of trade operations, the unreasonable restraining of marriages or the dealing in them as commercial bargains, and, perhaps, those wagering transactions which do not fall within the scope of the 5 and 6 Will. IV. c. 41[1]. The gaming transactions falling within the statute are not, as a rule, punishable *per se*, but they are expressly made *illegal* as considerations.

With regard to the effects of the rule, these differ according to the nature of the fault. An executory consideration which contemplates either illegality or immorality (as above defined) is not only worthless as a consideration, but will vitiate and render unenforceable the whole transaction. So that, even if the contract be under seal, and therefore capable of standing without any consideration at all, it will nevertheless be void[2]. The rule is the same if an executed consideration consists of an *illegal* act[3]. But, if the executed consideration be an *immoral* act, it will be treated merely as non-existent; and the contract, if otherwise unobjectionable, will be held simply as voluntary, and, if by specialty, enforceable at law[4].

11. *And the existence of an illegal or immoral consideration may be proved by external evidence, though the contract be embodied in writing, or even in a deed*[5].

This canon, an exception to the general rule

---

[1] cf. Anson, pp. 183—189. The other instances quoted by him are actual illegalities.

[2] Anson, pp. 187, 192. Leake, pp. 147, 631, 761. Pollock, pp. 288, 350.

[3] Leake, p. 760. Smith, p. 194.

[4] Anson, p. 178. Leake, p. 750. Pollock, p. 289. Smith, p. 196.

[5] Smith, p. 193. Addison, p. 501. Chitty, pp. 164, 673. Pollock, p. 356. Leake, p. 771. Anson, p. 49.

which refuses to admit parol testimony to vary or contradict the terms of a written instrument, is rendered necessary by the circumstances of the case. The general rule was devised to settle disputes between the parties, who may fairly be held to be concluded by their own deliberate expressions. But where the State is interested in prohibiting a course of conduct, it would be idle to allow such conduct to be practised under cover of fictitious language.

12. *In the case of executory considerations which fail or become impossible, the promisor will be wholly or partially released from his obligation, and may even recover back money paid under the contract.*

This canon appears to be a deduction from that principle of mutuality which is of the very essence of consideration. It is true that a promise, not less than a performance, may be a sufficient consideration. But this is, presumably, because the parties anticipate performance from promise. Where, therefore, it is clear that performance will not ensue, the consideration fails.

But it should be perfectly clear that the consideration must of necessity fail. It is not sufficient merely to form an estimate of the promisee's inability to carry it out. If *A* promises to give *X* lessons on the violin, in return for *X*'s promise to teach Latin to *A*'s son, and *A* dies, the contract is at an end, and *X* is discharged. And the same rule would, probably, hold, if *A* accepted an engagement which prevented him fulfilling his obligation. In the one case, the consideration would have become impossible; in the other, it would, in fact, fail. But it is conceived that a mere suspicion of A's intention to accept such an engagement, or in the case of a money consideration, a belief that the party liable was unable to discharge it, would not release the promisor, unless the performance of the consideration were expressly made a condition precedent to the performance of the promise.

But, with regard to the latter portion of the canon, the case is different. As a rule, the promisor who has paid money under the contract can only recover it back, as "money had and received," if the failure of consideration has been total. In the event of partial failure, his remedy is an action for damages. It is said, however, that if part of a severable and apportionable consideration fail wholly, a proportionate amount of money paid may be recovered[1].

It is now necessary to examine briefly the authorities on which these various canons are founded. Taking them again in the same order we get the following results;—

1. *Every true contract contains a promise. A consideration is a detriment voluntarily incurred by the promisee [or a benefit conferred on the promisor at the instance of the promisee] in exchange for the promise.*

The excessive caution of English judges has rendered them very reluctant to issue definitions. It is so rarely that a definition is essential to

---

[1] Chitty, pp. 87—93. Leake, pp. 103—114. Anson, pp. 299—308. Addison, pp. 232—234.

the decision of a case, it is so extremely improbable that the sternly practical minds of future judges will allow them to follow a definition at the expense of an inconsistent decision, that for a judge to commit himself to a definition is almost to invite criticism. Even in the case of such an important notion as *consideration*, we shall often find that what appears to be at first sight a definition, is, in fact, only a postulate.

For example, there arises at once the recent dictum of Lord Justice Lush in the case of *Currie v. Misa*[1]. "A valuable consideration, in the sense of the law, may consist either in some right, interest, profit, or benefit accruing to the one party, or some forbearance, detriment, loss; or responsibility, given, suffered, or undertaken by the other." This dictum, which is professedly founded on certain passages taken from Comyn's Digest[2], really leaves out of account one of the most vital qualities of a consideration, viz. its connection with the promise which it is intended to support. The deficiency is supplied by Lord Chelmsford[3], in moving the affirmance of Lord Justice Lush's judgment in the House of Lords. Lord Chelmsford speaks of the giving up of a document as—"undoubtedly a detriment to *Glyn and Co.*, which amounted in law to a sufficient consideration *moving from them for the cheque which was substituted for it.*" Here the essential mutuality of the consideration and the promise are clearly brought out.

[1] L. R. 10 Exch. 162.   [2] 5th ed. vol. I. p. 294.
[3] In *Misa v. Currie*, 1 App. Ca. 565.

The words of Mr Justice Patteson in the older
case of *Thomas v. Thomas*[1] are also well known.
"Consideration means something which is of some
value in the eye of the law, moving from the
plaintiff: it may be some benefit[2] to the plaintiff, or
some detriment[2] to the defendant, but at all events
it must be moving from the plaintiff." Even this
attempt at definition only supplies half the deficiency
left by Lord Justice Lush. It is not enough
that the consideration must "move from the plaintiff;" it must move from him *in contemplation of
the promise*. Otherwise the objections to past
consideration vanish. Mr Justice Patteson's judgment in this case is, however, valuable as helping to
explode the unscholarly and misleading doctrine,
which confuses the *causa* of Roman Law and the
cause of French Law with the English "consideration," which is, obviously, of an entirely different
character.

The mutuality of the consideration was clearly
in the mind of Lord Ellenborough when he delivered his judgment in the case of *Jones v.
Ashburnham*[3], decided in 1804. In that case the
plaintiff sued upon a debt originally due to him
from a person since deceased, which debt the defendant (probably the legal representative or, at any
rate, the relative of the deceased) had promised to

---

[1] 2 Q. B. 859.

[2] Surely these words should be transposed? Cf. opening
sentence of judgment of Le Blanc. J. in *Jones v. Ashburnham*,
4 East. 466.

[3] 4 East. 455.

pay. The plaintiff, in his declaration, alleged, as consideration for this promise, forbearance to sue, for some time, for the debt; and he also alleged that such forbearance had been accorded at the special instance and request of the defendant. But the declaration did not specify to whom the forbearance was accorded, nor did it appear on the pleadings that the defendant was liable, independently of her promise, to pay the debt. Lord Ellenborough said— "*Right* is a correlative term; there must be some object of right; some object of suit; some party who, in respect of some fund or some character known in the law, is liable; otherwise there cannot be said to be any *right*...Then what *forbearance* is shewn? It must be a *forbearance* of a right which may be enforced with effect[1]." And to the same effect Mr Justice Lawrence[2].

The difficulty, such as there was, in the case of *Jones v. Ashburnham*, appears to have arisen mainly from the expressions of Mr Justice Yates in the still earlier case of *Pillans v. Van Mierop*[3], a judgment which has since been decisively overruled on another point. In that case, the plaintiffs, *after giving credit to W*, wrote to the defendants, to know if they would honour bills drawn on them to meet *W*'s engagements. The defendants promised to do so, but, before fulfilling their promise, withdrew it. It will be noticed that the plaintiffs had not given *W* credit on the faith of the promise of the defen-

[1] 4 East, at p. 463.   [2] 4 East, at p. 466.
[3] 3 Burrow, 1664.

dants, and also that the defendants had not actually accepted the bills drawn on them. Nevertheless, the Court of King's Bench held the defendants liable; partly on the ground that such a promise needed no consideration[1], partly on the ground that a promise to accept was equal to an acceptance[2]. In this case, Mr Justice Yates said—"**Any** *damage* to another, or *suspension* or *forbearance* of his *right,* is a foundation for an undertaking, and will make it binding; though *no actual benefit* accrues to the party undertaking[3]." The fate which has attended this dictum may, perhaps, diminish our regret for the infrequency of judicial definitions.

But perhaps the most instructive authority of all is the masterly and incisive opinion delivered by Chief Baron Skynner to the House of Lords in the case of *Rann v. Hughes*[4], an opinion which has been preserved to the world almost, as it were, by accident. The Chief Baron's words are, that "the consideration must be coextensive with the promise," an expression which his subsequent language proves to mean—must be linked with it by unmistakeable ties. It must be in fact the immediately determining inducement to the promisor to undertake his liability. And this is perhaps as near as we can get to the

---

[1] 3 Burr. p. 1670. By Lord Mansfield; both on the ground that the promise was in writing, and that it was a mercantile transaction.

[2] 3 Burr. at p. 1673.

[3] p. 1674. This view of consideration was affirmed by the early case of *Williamson v. Clements* (1 Taunton, 522) in which Lord Mansfield acted as judge. But it is, of course, much older.

[4] 7 Term Reports, p. 350, *a.*

truth of the matter in judicial language, unless we adopt the words of Lord Denman in *Roscorla v. Thomas*[1], and say that "the promise must be coextensive with the consideration."

2. *Such consideration may be either the promise or the performance of an act or forbearance. If it be the performance, the consideration is said to be* **executed**; *if the promise, to be* **executory**.

It is apprehended that this canon hardly requires the quotation of any authority to support it. Every contract of service contains an example of the first class of considerations; in consideration that *A* promises to serve *B*, *B* promises to give *A* certain wages. Every action for the ordinary claim of "goods sold" affords an example of the latter class. But the distinction between the two classes is well brought out by the judgment of the Court of Common Pleas in the case of *The Fishmongers' Company v. Robertson*[2]. There the company entered into an agreement with the defendants, which agreement contained promises by the defendants given in consideration of certain promises by the company. The agreement, as originally framed, was not a contract; for, in order to render a corporation liable on its promise, the promise must be under the corporate seal. The alleged original consideration was, therefore, worthless. But the company performed its part of the agreement, and it was therefore able to set up a contract, of which the consideration was its performance of certain acts.

---

[1] 3 Q. B. at p. 237.
[2] 6 Scott. N. R. p. 56.

And this contract was held good. Nor can it be doubted that a forbearance, i.e. a conscious abstention from acts otherwise lawful, stands on the same footing as an act[1].

Unfortunately, the phraseology adopted to distinguish between these two classes of considerations is by no means uniform. The terms used by the most modern writers, viz. "executory" and "executed," are, or were until lately, often used by judges to distinguish between bilateral and unilateral *contracts*. Thus, in the case of *Foster v. Dawber*[2], Baron Parke said—"now, it is competent for both parties to an executory contract, by mutual agreement, without any satisfaction, to discharge the obligation of that contract. But an executed contract cannot be discharged except by release under seal, or by performance of the obligation." Here his Lordship is evidently distinguishing between contracts which contain mutual promises and contracts which leave nothing to be done by one party; and, though this distinction will square almost exactly with contracts founded on the respective classes of considerations, it is evident that the learned judge is thinking of the promise rather than the consideration. And this view is confirmed by the language of Chief Justice Tindal in the case previously quoted, *The Fishmongers' Company v. Robertson*.

---

[1] cf. *Smith v. Algar*, 1 B and Ad. 603. *Payne v. Wilson*, 7 B and C, 423. For an admirable example of executed consideration, see the recent case of *Carlill. v. Carbolic Smoke Ball Co.* [1892]. 2 Q. B. 484.

[2] 6 Exch. at p. 851.

" Even if the contract put in suit by the corporation had been on their part executory only, not executed, we feel little doubt but that their suing upon the contract would amount to an admission" etc.[1]. And the Chief Justice had used similar language in a similar case of *Arnold v. The Mayor of Poole*[2], decided a year previously.

But, in both these cases, the same learned judge shewed by his expressions that the terms were still in a state of uncertain application. In the first, *Arnold v. The Mayor of Poole*[2], he speaks of the liability of a municipal corporation upon a consideration which "had been executed;" in the second, he speaks of a promise implied by law on an "executed consideration[3]."

Unhappily, however, the term "executed" even as applied to considerations, has undergone a change of meaning during the present century. The pivot case is *Thornton v. Jenyns*[4], decided in 1840, in which the same learned judge whose words we have previously quoted (Chief Justice Tindal) took part. *Thornton v. Jenyns* was a case in which a promise was alleged to rest upon a consideration "that the plaintiff *had then* promised the defendants to observe" etc. Mr Justice Bosanquet, agreeing with the Chief Justice, said[5] "It is contended on the part of the defendants, that the promise is founded upon a past consideration. No doubt, a consideration that is *completely executed and gone by* is not a

[1] 6 Scott N. R. at p. 105. [2] 4 M. and G. at p. 895.
[3] 6 Scott N. R. at p. 107. [4] 1 Scott N. R. p. 52.
[5] at p. 75.

sufficient consideration for a promise." And again—
"Now, it is said that this promise of the plaintiff,
......appears upon the record to have been made
antecedently to the defendant's promise; *that it
was an executed or past consideration*, and therefore
insufficient to support the subsequent promise[1]."
But the learned judge then proceeded to hold that
the allegation was "that, upon the same occasion,
and at the same time, the parties mutually promised
to perform the agreement[2]," while Mr Justice
Coltman, who followed, held the promises upon
which the action was brought to have been simultaneous[3]; and, therefore, unobjectionable on the
ground of consideration. No doubt, the consideration
in question was in any case "executory" in the
modern sense, but the importance of the expressions
quoted lies in the fact that the Court is evidently
feeling its way towards the distinction between a
promise which is really voluntary, though prompted
by a bygone service, and a promise which is the
immediate result of a service which has just been
rendered—where, in fact, the offer of the promisor
has preceded the performance by the promisee.

The older cases certainly speak of "executed"
where we should now speak of "past" considerations.
Lord Denman in *Eastwood v. Kenyon* (1840)[4], Lord
Abinger in *Hopkins v. Logan* (1839)[5], Baron Parke
in *King v. Sears* (1835)[6], all adopt this view; and
although in *Streeter v. Horlock* (1822)[7] there was a

[1] 1 Scott, p. 75.   [2] p. 76.
[3] p. 78.   [4] 11 A. and E. at p. 451.
[5] 5 M. and W. at p. 247.   [6] 2 C. M. and R at p. 53.
[7] 1 Bingham at p. 37.

faint anticipation of modern practice, the language is not sufficiently clear to found safe conclusions. In the still older cases—*Lampleigh v. Brathwait* (1615)[1], *Sidenham v. Worlington* (1584)[2], and *Hunt v. Bate* (1567)[3]—"executed" consideration was clearly "past" consideration. In *Sidenham v. Worlington*, Periam, J. brings out admirably the necessary mutuality of promise and consideration. But these older cases naturally belong to a subsequent chapter.

3. *The existence of a consideration is essential to the validity of every " simple " or formless contract, i. e. every contract not contained in sealed writing nor apparent on the records of a Court of Justice.*

Since the emphatic language of Chief Baron Skynner, in *Rann v. Hughes*[4], this proposition, in its more obvious meaning, has been undisputable. "The law of this country," said the Chief Baron, "supplies no means, nor affords any remedy, to compel the performance of an agreement made without sufficient consideration." Alluding to the doctrine broached by the judges in the earlier case of *Pillans v. Van Mierop*[5], he added[6]—"All contracts are, by the laws of England, distinguished into agreements by specialty, and agreements by parol, nor is there any such third class as some of the counsel have endeavoured to maintain, as contracts in writing. If they be merely written and not specialties, they are parol, and a con-

---

[1] Hobart at p. 105.
[2] 2 Leonard 224.
[3] Dyer, fo. 272 *b*.
[4] 7 T. R. 350, *n*.
[5] 3 Burr. 1663.
[6] 7 T. R. p. 351, *n*.

sideration must be proved." And the Chief Baron distinctly repudiated the doctrine that the imposition of additional requirements by the Statute of Frauds impliedly did away with the older necessity for a consideration. Inasmuch as the so-called "contracts of record" are not really contracts at all, the opinion of the Chief Baron, which was adopted by all the judges and by the Lords in the case of *Rann v. Hughes*[1], and has been received as good law ever since, covers the whole of the canon which we are here endeavouring to assert.

But there is one special application of the canon which appears to be viewed with some suspicion by at least one writer of repute. This is the application which insists upon a consideration for the parol release of a contract. Since the decision of the House of Lords in *Foakes v. Beer*[2], it must be admitted that the doctrine is good modern law. In that case the plaintiff was entitled to a certain sum on a previous judgment for which the defendant was liable, and she voluntarily agreed to accept a smaller sum in discharge. The agreement was in writing and undisputed. But the House of Lords, affirming the Court of Appeal, held that it was invalid to create a binding contract. And though the great authority of Lord Blackburn wavered, the other judges were clear as to the

---

[1] 7 T. R. 350. But it will be noticed that the judges in the case of *Michinson v. Hewson*, which gave rise to the report of *Rann v. Hughes*, edged away from the Chief Baron's doctrine, preferring to rest their decision on a technical point.

[2] L. R. 9, App. Ca. 605.

existence of the doctrine, which, it is submitted, would hold, *à fortiori*, where the agreement was for unconditional discharge.

It is somewhat difficult to see cause for the unpopularity of the doctrine. It is surely no more unreasonable to insist that a man shall not throw away an advantage which he possesses without some compensation, than it is to insist that he shall not bind himself to a liability without some return. In both cases he does in fact part with an advantage. The difference is mainly one of form. Nevertheless, the doctrine is distinctly unpopular. One of its most famous developements, that asserted in *Cumber v. Wane*[1], which refused to allow a negotiable instrument for £5 to form the consideration for a parol release of a liability for £15, has been overruled, or at least dissented from, by the later decision of *Sibree v. Tripp*[2]; and the very modern case of *Bidder v. Bridges*[3], in the Court of Appeal, has decided that a mere cheque, at any rate if it is not the defendant's cheque, though for a smaller amount, will release the liability for a larger, if accepted with that understanding. The slightly earlier decision in *Goddard v. O'Brien*[4], which, however, was not before the Court of Appeal, took the same view with regard to the defendant's own cheque.

The main doctrine, however, is clear. We have now to consider an interesting corollary springing from it.

[1] 1 Strange, 426.
[2] 15 M. and W. 23.
[3] 37 Ch. D. 406.
[4] 9 Q. B. D. 37.

Where by any rule of law an agreement must be reduced to writing as a condition precedent to becoming a contract, the consideration must appear in the writing if in fact it was stated in the agreement.

This is only another way of saying that the consideration is an integral part of every simple contract, and not merely an external appendage. Such was the view taken by Lord Ellenborough in the leading case of *Wain v. Warlters*[1], which, though the actual point it decided has ceased to be important (by reason of recent legislation), is still a binding authority in analogous cases. *Wain v. Warlters* decided that, inasmuch as an agreement of guarantee was required by the Statute of Frauds to be evidenced by written note or memorandum, to entitle it to rank as a contract, the consideration of such agreement must appear in the writing. Mr Justice Lawrence put it thus:—"As the consideration for the promise is part of the agreement, that ought also to be stated in writing[2]." And the rule in *Wain v. Warlters* has since been followed in the cases of *Saunders v. Wakefield* (1821)[3], *Raikes v. Todd* (1838)[4], and, by implication, in *Oldershaw v. King* (1857)[5]. The only relaxation of any importance is that introduced by the judges in the case of *Johnston v. Nicholls* (1845)[6], and adopted in *Oldershaw v. King*[7] by Chief Baron Pollock, whose dissentient judgment was afterwards upheld by the

---

[1] 5 East, 10.
[2] 5 East, at p. 19.
[3] 4 B. and Ald. 595.
[4] 8 A. and E. 846.
[5] 2 H. and N. 517.
[6] 1 C. B. 251.
[7] 2 H. and N. at p. 406.

Exchequer Chamber[1],—that the statement of the consideration need not be express; it is sufficient if it can be gathered from the general sense of the documents. An earlier case of *Russell v. Moseley*[2] appears to be quite inconsistent with *Wain v. Warlters*. Apparently there would be no objection to the oral proof of consideration for a contract the other terms of which were, as a matter of fact, but without legal necessity, expressed in writing, unless the writing negatived the idea of such consideration[3].

The operation of this corollary has, however, been expressly abolished by statute[4] in the case of guarantees, on which most of the old decisions turned; and, by the custom of merchants, long since incorporated into English law, it is settled that the consideration neither for the making nor for the discharge of a negotiable instrument need be stated in writing[5], though all other essential terms must appear in the instrument[6]. But between the making and the discharge of a negotiable instrument there is this important distinction, that the former requires a consideration, though it need not be stated[7], while the latter needs no consideration at all[8]. Moreover, the presumption is always in favour of the existence of a consideration for a negotiable

---

[1] 2 H. and N. 517.   [2] 6 Moore 521.

[3] *Allen v. Pink*, 4 M. and W. 140.

[4] 19 and 20 Vic. c. 97.

[5] 45 and 46 Vic. c. 61, §§ 30, 62 and 63.

[6] 45 and 46 Vic. c. 61, §§ 3 and 83.

[7] 45 and 46 Vic. c. 61, § 28 (2), inference.

[8] 45 and 46 Vic. c. 61, § 62.

instrument, until it is proved to be tainted with irregularity[1]. This presumption does not, of course, exist in the case of a guarantee.

But the final clause of the corollary has introduced a much more doubtful class of exceptions to the general rule. It must now be taken as decided, though the last case appears to be no later than the year 1834[2], that where the amount of the consideration has not been expressly agreed on by the parties, and it is therefore left to be fixed by market rate, or the opinion of a jury, the absence of all reference to it in the writing is no objection, at least under the 17th section of the Statute of Frauds. And there seems no reason of principle why the same rule should not apply to agreements falling under the 4th section, or other statutes. There have indeed been attempts to distinguish between the "agreement" of section 4, and the "bargain" of section 17[3]; but such attempts are hardly dignified. The objection to the whole doctrine of the exception, is, as before pointed out, that it encourages oral proof of circumstances which the Statute of Frauds declined to credit on the memory of witnesses; and thereby facilitates a course of action clean contrary to the policy of the statute[4].

---

[1] 45 and 46 Vic. c. 61, § 38 (2).

[2] *Hoadly v. McLaine.* 10 Bingham, 482.

[3] e.g. by Lord Ellenborough and Lawrence, J. in *Egerton v. Matthews*, 6 East, 307.

[4] It may be regarded as a point of some nicety whether an unsigned deed would satisfy the requirements of the 4th section of the Statute of Frauds. The judges in *Cherry v. Heming* (4 Exch. 631) thought that it would, or, rather, that the statute did not

4. *In certain cases a consideration is essential also to the validity of a contract under seal, and in nearly all cases it is a condition precedent to the granting of the special remedy of " specific performance."*

The first part of this canon applies chiefly to the cases of "covenants in restraint of trade" i.e. covenants in some way restraining the covenantor from pursuing a lawful calling. It is well known that such covenants were looked upon with great disfavour during the Middle Ages, and in the earlier cases, as will hereafter be seen, the usual course was to treat the covenant as absolutely null. In many instances, this undiscriminating condemnation led to practical inconvenience. It rendered businesses unsaleable, and made employers unwilling to take apprentices.

The first authoritative declaration of the modern and more reasonable doctrine appears to have come from the judges of the Court of King's Bench in the case of *Mitchel v. Reynolds*[1], decided in the year 1711. It is, therefore, to the Common Law Courts, and not to the Court of Chancery, that we owe this beneficial piece of judicial legislation[2]; for the earlier cases referred to on this point by Chief

---

apply to transactions evidenced by deed. But the point was not decided. And, clearly, the reasoning in *Wain v. Warlters* would not require the statement of the consideration.

[1] 1 Peere Williams (6th ed.), 181.

[2] That the doctrine was of Common Law origin, was recognized by the Court of Chancery, when it sent a case involving it to the Court of King's Bench for opinion. *Bunn v. Guy*, 4 East 190.

Justice Parker in *Mitchel v. Reynolds*[1] are, with much deference be it said, not authorities for his doctrine at all. Those[2] in which the question of consideration was raised, were cases of *assumpsit* on simple contract, where a consideration was material on general principles. Indeed, in one case to which the learned Chief Justice refers, that of *Barrow v. Wood*[3], Mr Justice Reeve went so far as to declare *all* bonds in restraint of trade to be void. " A man " (says he) " may contract or promise that he will not use his Trade, but he cannot bind himself in a bond not to do it, for if he do so, it is void[4]."

Chief Justice Parker then must be credited, much against his will, with the authorship of the modern doctrine. His judgment in *Mitchel v. Reynolds* is a masterpiece of old legal style, and covers the whole ground of the " restraint of trade " doctrine. After dealing with statutory and customary restrictions, he proceeds to divide voluntary restraints, or restraints by agreement of the parties, into " general " (those which stipulate for a total abstinence from any trade) and " particular " (those which restrain its exercise for a limited time or within certain localities). After denouncing the former as bad under all circumstances, he includes in the same condemnation " particular restraints

---

[1] 1 P. W. 185.

[2] e.g. *Broad v. Jollyffe.* Cro. Jac. 596 (reported as *Joliffe v. Brode* in W. Jones, 13, and as *Jelliet v. Broad* in Noy 98), and *Prugnell v. Gosse*, Aleyn, 67. The case of *Hunlocke v. Blacklowe* (2 Saunders, 155) turned upon a purely technical point.

[3] March, 191.   [4] at p. 193.

without consideration, all which are void by what sort of contract soever created[1]." But, he adds, " where a contract for restraint of trade" (meaning a "particular" restraint) "appears to be made upon a good and adequate consideration, so as to make it a proper and useful contract, it is good." And, this being the precise case before the Court, the decision of the Chief Justice must be regarded as a binding precedent.

It was soon followed by a string of cases[2] which relied so closely on its wording as to give rise for a short time to an inconvenient doctrine, afterwards abandoned. It will be noticed that the Chief Justice, in *Mitchel v. Reynolds,* uses the phrase "good *and adequate* consideration." Hence arose the theory that the Court was bound to consider, not merely the existence of the consideration, but also its adequacy. *Young v. Timmins*[3] (1831) was a case in which the defendants had agreed to employ one Ireland "as heretofore," without specifying other terms, and, in consideration of the employment, Ireland agreed not to work for any other person outside a radius of six miles from London, without the consent of the defendants. The Court of Exchequer held the consideration not to be adequate. " The question then, in the present case," said Lord Lyndhurst[4], " is, whether there is an adequate consideration for the stipulations in this agreement

[1] 1 P. W. p. 185.

[2] e.g. *Chesman v. Nainby* (affirmed in Lords), 2 Strange 739. *Bunn v. Guy,* 4 East, 190. *Gale v. Reed,* 8 East, 79 *n.*

[3] 1 Cr. and J. 331.   [4] at p. 339.

on the part of the bankrupt" (Ireland)......"It does appear to me that this coupled with the other clauses, places *Ireland* entirely at the mercy of the *Messrs Timmins*, and that there is no adequate consideration for this agreement to work exclusively for the defendants." And the other judges took the same view. It is true that *Young v. Timmins* was a case of parol agreement, though no point was made of the fact. But in the same year the Court of Common Pleas applied the same doctrine to a specialty contract. In the case of *Horner v. Graves*[1], Chief Justice Tindal, delivering the judgment of the Court, said[2]—"But the question is, whether this contract, which is in particular and partial restraint of trade only, *and is made upon some consideration, is made upon a good and sufficient consideration.*" And, having examined the question, he adds—"Surely this appears a very slender and inadequate consideration for such a sacrifice." It is remarkable, however, that, in this very case, the Chief Justice foreshadowed the later doctrine on the subject. It is not the adequacy of the consideration but the reasonableness of the restriction that the Court is now concerned with. And this reasonableness is not only in respect of the party himself (in which case the adequacy of the consideration would be a valuable guide) but also in respect of the public interests. "But the greater question is whether this is a reasonable restraint of trade; and we do not see how a better test can be applied to the

---

[1] 5 M. and P. 768.   [2] at p. 781.

question, whether reasonable or not, than by considering whether the restraint is such only as to afford a fair protection to the interests of the party in favour of whom it is given, and not so large as to interfere with the interests of the public......Whatever is injurious to the interests of the public is void, on the grounds of public policy[1]."

Six years after the decision in *Horner v. Graves*, the doctrine foreshadowed by Chief Justice Tindal was applied by the Exchequer Chamber in the case of *Hitchcock v. Coker*[2]. In that case the same learned judge, delivering the judgment of the Exchequer Chamber, emphatically disclaimed the doctrine that the Court was bound to weigh the adequacy of the consideration. " But if by adequacy of consideration more is intended, and that the Court must weigh whether the consideration is equal in value to that which the party gives up or loses by the restraint under which he has placed himself, we feel ourselves bound to differ from that doctrine[3]." And this is the view adopted by the recent cases[4]—that if there *be* consideration, its adequacy is not material: that the question for the Court is the reasonableness of the restriction, regard being had to the objects of the arrangement and the

---

[1] 5 M. and P. 782, 783.

[2] 6 A. and E. 438.

[3] 6 A. and E. at p. 456.

[4] e.g. *Allsopp v. Wheatcroft* L. R. 15 Eq. 59. *Collins v. Locke* 4 App. Ca. 674. *Rousillon v. Rousillon* 14 Ch. D. 351. *Mineral Water Society v. Booth*, 36 Ch. D. 465, &c.

interests of the public. But this point does not come within our subject [1].

We have now to notice that the absence of a consideration from a specialty contract may, in certain cases, impair its value, though it does not render it void. For example, in the administration of the estate of a deceased person by the Court, the claimant under an obligation entered into without consideration by the deceased, even though the obligation be contained in a sealed instrument, is postponed to all the creditors for consideration, even though their claims are not supported by specialty [2].

Again, the absence of a consideration is usually a fatal bar to an application for the remedy of specific performance. The caution of the older judges of the Court of Chancery laid down the wise maxim that this important remedy can never be demanded as a matter of course; and that the Court must be perfectly clear that the party to whom it is granted has, not merely clean hands, but a clear conscience. This doctrine, as applied to want of consideration, is, perhaps comparatively modern, but it can certainly be traced back beyond the commencement of the present century. In the case of *Colman v. Sarrel* [3] Lord Thurlow said—"The difficulty is to show a

---

[1] At this stage it may be noticed that the presence of a consideration, may, if coupled with *bona fides*, save a specialty contract which would otherwise be void under section 48 of the Bankruptcy Act 1883 (46 and 47 Vic. c. 52). And see the general protection to contracts for valuable consideration, afforded by section 49.

[2] Cf. e.g. *Clough v. Lambert*, 10 Sim. 179. *Watson v. Parker*, 6 Beav. 288. *Hales v. Cox*, 32 Beav. 121.

[3] 1 Vesey Jun. 52.

case where any voluntary gift has been executed in Equity," and, again; "the Court has never yet executed a voluntary agreement[1]." And the rule has been consistently followed by a series of cases— *Ellison v. Ellison* (1802)[2], *Antrobus v. Smith* (1806)[3], *Groves v. Groves* (1829)[4], *Walrond v. Walrond* (1858)[5], and *Kennedy v. May* (1863)[6],—which place it beyond question[7].

But in certain other cases the doctrines of the Court are not by any means so clear. There was, for instance, long a theory that specific performance of a contract would not be decreed where the consideration was *inadequate*. In the old case of *Savile v. Savile*[8], decided in 1721, not even the rare spectacle of a former Lord Chancellor pleading at the bar of his successor could induce the latter to decree specific performance of a contract for sale of land so burdensome to the purchaser that he was ready to forfeit a thousand pounds rather than complete it. And this, notwithstanding that the contract had been entered into with the officer of the Court, and

---

[1] 1 Vesey Jun. at p. 55.   [2] 6 Vesey, 661.
[3] 12 Vesey, 45.   [4] 3 Yo. and J. 170.
[5] Johnson, 24 and 25.   [6] 11 W. R. 359.

[7] There is, however, one apparent exception to the rule, in the case of family arrangements. In these instances (to quote the words of Lord Hardwicke in *Stapilton v. Stapilton*, 1 Atkyns at p. 11) " a court of equity will be glad to lay hold of any just ground to carry (the agreement) into execution." And the plaintiff had a decree, although there was really no valuable consideration. See also the doctrine affirmed in *Stephens v. Trueman*, 1 Vesey Sen. 74, *Smith v. Mogford*, 21 W. R. 472.

[8] 1 Peere Williams, 744.

there was no suspicion of fraud. And in *Day v. Newman*[1], where there was great inadequacy of consideration, but no fraud or undue haste, Lord Alvanley, though he refused to rescind the contract, equally declined to grant a decree for specific performance.

Later authorities, however, have thrown great doubt upon the rule laid down by Lord Macclesfield in *Savile v. Savile*. In the well-known case of *Coles v. Trecothick*, Lord Eldon said—" But, farther, unless the inadequacy of price is such as shocks the conscience, and amounts in itself to conclusive and decisive evidence of fraud in the transaction, it is not itself a sufficient ground for refusing a specific performance[2]." And this view was followed, though with some obscurity of language, in *Sworder v. Abbott*[3], decided in 1851.

A similar fate has befallen the old rule on the subject of the sale of reversionary interests, which has now been regulated by statute. So strong was the presumption that a man would not part with an interest of this character unless he were, financially or morally, *in extremis*, that the Courts conceived themselves bound to protect the vendor in every way. Not only would they refuse a decree for specific performance on the simple ground of inadequacy of price[4], (a matter really very difficult

---

[1] 2 Cox, 77.   [2] 9 Vesey, 246.

[3] 4 De G. and S. 448. See also *Hammond v. Cope*, 25 Beav. 153.

[4] *Davies v. The Duke of Marlborough*, 2 Swanst., 143. *Playford v. Playford* (1845), 4 Hare, 551.

to ascertain), but they cast upon the purchaser the burden of proving the adequacy[1], thereby, in effect, raising a presumption of fraud. These rules were not, however, applied in cases in which the circumstances negatived all possibility of over-reaching, as, for example, when the reversion was sold by public auction[2]. And they have (presumably) been abolished by the 31 Vic. c. 4, which provides that "No Purchase, made *bonâ fide* and without fraud or unfair dealing, of any Reversionary Interest in Real or Personal Estate shall hereafter be opened or set aside merely on the Ground of Undervalue[3]." For, though the section does not expressly refer to the subject of specific performance, its meaning would be seriously impaired by any refusal of the Courts to aid with their most effective machinery purchasers who relied upon it.

5. *But, in the cases contemplated by Canon 4, the consideration need not be stated in the deed.*

The reason of this doctrine has already been explained; it only remains now to shew the authority for it. There is direct authority both for the narrower and the wider assertions of the canon. In the cases of restraint of trade, the Court has allowed the consideration to be proved *aliunde*[4]; and it has followed the same rule when the claim for

[1] *Gowland v. De Faria*, 17 Vesey 24. *Hincksman v. Smith*, 3 Russell 435.

[2] *Shelly v. Nash*, 3 Maddock, 232.

[3] 31 Vic. c. 4, § 1. The word "purchase" is expressly made to include a contract for purchase, (§ 3).

[4] *Rousillon v. Rousillon*, 14 Ch. D. 351. *Mineral Water Society v. Booth*, 36 Ch. D. 465.

specific performance has been resisted[1]. But the broader proposition has also been affirmed, that a consideration not inconsistent with the terms of a deed may always be proved by parol. In the old case of *Rex v. Scammonden*[2], a purchase deed stated the consideration as £28, and the Court allowed it to be shewn that the true consideration was £34. 4*s*. In *Leifchild's Case*[3], where a deed stated a nominal consideration, a person not a party to it was allowed to prove the true consideration. In *Townend v. Toker*[4], terms which formed the real consideration of an apparently voluntary deed of settlement were proved by external evidence. And in the recent case of *Llanelly Railway Co. v. London and North-Western Railway Co.*[5] the Court of Appeal allowed proof of a loan of £40,000, as part of the consideration for an agreement under seal in which no mention of it was made. But, presumably, the party to a deed would not be allowed to shew consideration absolutely inconsistent with its statements; nor would the absence of a consideration be passed over, where the agreement on which the deed was founded was required by law to be stated in writing.

6. *In accordance with the general rule of law, the onus of proving the existence of a consideration usually rests upon the party setting up the contract, whether the consideration appears in writing or not. But, in the case of negotiable instruments, the existence*

---

[1] *Clifford v. Turrell*, 1 Yo. and C. (N. R.) 149.

[2] 3 T. R. 474.   [3] L. R. 1 Eq. 231.

[4] L. R. 1 Ch. App. 446.   [5] L. R. 8 Ch. App. 942.

*of consideration is presumed, in the absence of sus-
picious circumstances.*

The main assertion of this canon, being so obviously within the rule implied in the maxim *omnia
contra proferentem*, hardly needs proof. Consideration being essential to the existence of a parol
contract, the party who asserts that there is a
contract must prove consideration in the course of
proving his assertion. To this rule there is one
important exception, in the case of negotiable instruments. It has long been law, not only that
the original contract must be presumed to have
been for value, but also that subsequent transfers
of it by delivery or indorsement raise the same presumption. This doctrine was explicitly laid down
by Chief Justice Eyre in *Collins v. Martin*[1] (decided
in 1797), accepted by Chief Justice Abbot in *Holliday
v. Atkinson* (1826)[2], and made statute law by the
"Bills of Exchange Act 1882[3]."

But an attempt has been made to carry the rule
still further, and to assert that in a contract by
specialty a consideration will be presumed unless
the contrary appears, or, as it is generally put, that
" a deed imports a consideration." To this assertion
several eminent writers on the law of evidence
commit themselves[4]. But the only judicial authority quoted by them for the rule—the case of

[1] 1 B. and P. at p. 651. [2] 5 B. and C. at p. 503.
[3] 45 and 46 Vic. c. 61, §§ 30 and 89.
[4] Starkie (3rd ed.), III. p. 930. Pitt Taylor (8th ed.), I. 110.
Best (7th ed.), p. 221. Doubtless founded on the observations of
judges, e.g. *Mitchel v. Reynolds*, 1 P. W. at p. 192.

Lowe v. Peers[1]—certainly does not bear it out; and it seems clear that the *dicta* of the text-book writers only amount to an incorrect way of saying that a consideration is not in general necessary to a contract by specialty. For it is undoubtedly true that in those cases in which the law does require consideration for a promise under seal, the *onus* of proving the existence of the consideration lies upon the party seeking to enforce the promise. For example, the 8th section of the Bills of Sale Act 1878[2] requires that every Bill of Sale shall state the consideration for which it was given, and the 8th section of the amending Act of 1882 requires that such consideration shall be duly set forth in the instrument[3]. It can hardly be doubted that under these statutes the person claiming under a Bill of Sale is bound to prove the correctness of the statement, and, thereby, the existence of a consideration, which, by the Act of 1882, in the case of every Bill of Sale given to secure the payment of money[4], must amount at least to the sum of £30[5]. And although it is hard to find any actual decision on the point, the language of the judges clearly goes to shew that the *onus* of proving the existence of the consideration required (even in a specialty contract) for a restraint of trade, falls on the party seeking to enforce the restraint.

---

[1] 4 Burr. 2225. Neither does *Shubrick v. Salmond* (3 Burr. 1637), quoted by May, p. 401.

[2] 41 and 42 Vic. c. 31, § 8.

[3] 45 and 46 Vic. c. 43.   [4] § 3.

[5] § 12. And cf. *Cochrane v. Moore*, 25 Q. B. D. 57.

7. *In ordinary cases, it is immaterial whether or no the consideration be economically adequate to the promise.*

This assertion, like the last, is almost too clear to need proof. We have already seen that the Courts have abandoned the doctrine of adequacy in the cases of restraint of trade. It is hardly to be supposed, therefore, that in ordinary cases, where there is no suspicion of illegality (for it cannot be said to be illegal to enter into an agreement without consideration) there would be any inclination to favour the stricter rule. Judges have, over and over again, disclaimed any intention of enquiring into the adequacy of a consideration. One of the best known cases is that of *Bainbridge v. Firmstone*[1], where the consideration alleged was the permission given to the defendant by the plaintiff to weigh two boilers belonging to the plaintiff. The modern, as opposed to the historical ground of the decision, was thus stated by Patteson, J.—"At any rate, there is a detriment to the plaintiff from his parting with possession for even so short a time[2]." In the "accord and satisfaction" cases, the addition of the hat or other trifle, which cures the defect of the gratuitous release, shews how immaterial is the economic adequacy to the validity of the contract. And, even with regard to the special remedies of equity, although it used to be held that inadequacy of consideration entitled the Court to refuse to grant

---

[1] 8 A. and E. 743.
[2] 8 A. and E. at p. 744.

them, it has been seen to be now the accepted doctrine that mere inadequacy is not sufficient[1].

8. *But gross inadequacy of consideration, though in itself no objection to the validity of a contract, either at law or in equity, may be evidence of fraud.*

This was the view expressed by Lord Eldon in the case of *Stilwell v. Wilkins*[2]. There a common sailor was induced to sell the fee simple of land worth at least £189 per annum for a sum of £250 down and an annuity of 50 guineas. Other circumstances were alleged, but, owing to the deaths of both the parties to the transaction, it was very difficult to prove them. The Vice-Chancellor made an order for a receiver in a suit to set aside the purchase, and the Chancellor, confirming the order said—"It is most certain that in general a sale will not be set aside on that ground" (i.e. inadequacy of price); "yet there may be cases of inadequacy so enormously great as to form a ground for cancelling the contract[3]." And in *Cockell v. Taylor*[4], decided in the year 1852, Lord Romilly (M. R.) said—"It" (inadequacy of price) "is in fact evidence of fraud, but, standing alone, by no means conclusive evidence." And the purchase was there set aside at the instance of the purchaser. But, as early as the year 1787, the Court of Exchequer, in its equity jurisdiction, had declined to receive inadequacy of consideration

---

[1] *Coles v. Trecothick*, 9 Vesey, 246. *Burrowes v. Lock*, 10 Vesey 474. *Abbott v. Sworder*, 4 De G. and Sm. 456.

[2] Jacob, p. 280.   [3] Jacob, p. 280.

[4] 15 Beav. at p. 115.

as *conclusive* evidence of fraud[1], and, in 1802, Lord Eldon, though the point did not then arise for actual decision, expressed his views in the same direction[2]. The language of the same learned judge, however, in the subsequent cases of *Underhill v. Horwood*[3] and *Mortlock v. Buller*[4], is by no means free from ambiguity. In each of these cases, except the last, there had been, not merely a contract, but also a conveyance, and the subject of conveyances will be considered later on. Meanwhile it is not perhaps too much to say that the state of the authorities, on the subject of inadequacy as evidence of fraud, is not entirely satisfactory[5].

9. *On the other hand, the consideration must be genuine.*

In the discussion of the judicial authorities for this canon, we may as well follow the order of detail adopted in our treatment of the text-book doctrines.

First, then, an act or promise, which, though apparently a benefit to the promisor, is not really of any advantage to him, will not be a genuine consideration. This is the language of old decisions, and it has been accepted without question in modern times. Thus, where the consideration was alleged to be the promise of forbearance to sue *per paululum tempus*[6],

---

[1] *Griffith v. Spralley*, Cox, 389.

[2] In *White v. Damon*, 7 Vesey, 1 at p. 35.

[3] 10 Vesey, 219.   [4] 10 Vesey, 311.

[5] See these collected in Chitty's *Equity Index* (4th ed.) sub. tit. *Specific Performance, Defences to suits for*, VI.

[6] *Trickett v. Marrdlee*, Siderfin, 45, disapproving an earlier case (*Cooks v. Douze* Cro. Car. 241) where a contrary doctrine had been held.

or *pro aliquo tempore*[1], the action of assumpsit was not allowed, even though actual forbearance in pursuance of the promise was averred. So, too, the creation[2] or the surrender[3] of an estate at will which the promisor was admittedly entitled to determine at pleasure. And where a man promised to discharge a debt owing by *E*'s husband, *for which she was not liable*, this was held no consideration for a promise by *E*[4]. But, although the consideration is of no advantage to the promisor, if it is a real detriment to the promisee, and given in exchange for the promise, it is, of course, genuine.

The converse case occurs where the consideration, though apparently detrimental to the promisee, is not really so; as, for example, when the latter promises to do, or actually does, something which he was legally liable to the promisor to do. Thus in the leading case of *Stilk v. Meyrick*[5], which, though only a *Nisi Prius* decision, has since been followed by the decisions in *Harris v. Carter* (1854)[6] and *Frazer v. Halton* (1857)[7], a seaman who refused to continue his legal duty of serving on board ship unless the master would agree to raise his wages, was held unable to recover on the contract to pay increased wages in return for continued service,

---

[1] *Tolson v. Clerk*, Cro. Car. 438. But a promise to forbear for a *reasonable* time, has been said to be consideration. *Oldershaw v. King*, 2 H. and N. 517, questioning *Semple v. Pink*, 1 Exch. 74.

[2] *Keble's case*, quoted in *Beven v. Cowling*, 1 Poph. 183.

[3] *Kent v. Prat*, Brownlowe I. 6 (badly reported).

[4] *Westbie v. Cockaine*, referred to in 1 Viner Abr. 311.

[5] 2 Campbell at p. 318.   [6] 3 E. and B. 559.

[7] 2 C. B., N. S. at p. 525.

because there was no consideration for it. Similarly, a promise by a tenant, under liability to repair the premises, to fulfil his obligation, was held no consideration[1]. And on the same reasoning a release of an alleged interest, to which in fact the releasor is not entitled, is no consideration[2]—the detriment is only apparent, not real. But it has been held that, where a man engages himself to perform for *B* a duty which he is already bound to perform for *A*, or, in other words, gives a second person the right to enforce the performance of the same act, this engagement will be valid as a consideration[3]. It is quite possible that the old rule of law, which prevented the assignment of a *chose in action* without the consent of the party liable, is accountable for this rather refined distinction; and it will be interesting to see whether the recent abolition of that rule[4] will make any difference in the doctrine.

Again, so-called "moral consideration" is not genuine, mainly, it is suggested, because the vital element of *exchange* is wanting in it. A "moral consideration" is said to arise when the existence of a particular state of circumstances creates an inclination in the promisor to assist the promisee. Thus, when there is a near blood relationship between promisor and promisee, and the latter is in such a situation that the world regards him as having a

[1] *Bayley v. Homan*, 3 Bing. N. C. 915.

[2] *Kaye v. Dutton*, 7 M. and G. at p. 817.

[3] *Scotson v. Pegg*, 6 H. and N. 295. *Shadwell v. Shadwell*, 9 C. B., N. S. 159.

[4] By the Judicature Act, 1873, § 25 (6).

conventional claim to a benefit from the promisor, a
promise by the latter is said to rest on a moral consideration. For this special class of considerations
some writers and judges reserve the special term
" good," to distinguish them from economic considerations, which they term " valuable." But the
practice is uncertain and confusing. Whatever may
be the virtue of " good" considerations as supporting
conveyances (a point to be dealt with hereafter), it
has long been settled law that a " good" consideration
will not uphold a simple contract[1].

But there are moral considerations other than
those arising out of blood relationship, and there
used to be a theory that some of these were sufficient
to support a simple contract. Thus, in the case of
Hawkes v. Saunders[2], Lord Mansfield said, with
the concurrence of the whole Court of King's Bench,
" Where a man is under a moral obligation, which
no court of law or equity can enforce, and *promises*,
the honesty and rectitude of the thing is a consideration." And the Court gave judgment for the
payment of a legacy by an executrix who had
promised (having assets) to pay it, although the
declaration would not have been sufficient to support
the claim apart from the promise, and there was no
economic consideration for the undertaking. Expressions apparently approving of this doctrine are

---

[1] Bacon, (Montagu ed.) XIII. p. 182, (Law Tracts, Reg. XVIII).
Modern authorities practically use the terms " good " and " valu-
able " indiscriminately, as for example Cotton, L. J. in *Miles v.
New Zealand Estate Co.* (32 Ch. D. at p. 283.)

[2] Cowper, 290.

to be found in *Atkins v. Banwell*[1], and other cases[2], but it is clear that it is not now law. The strong case of *Eastwood v. Kenyon*[3], decided in 1840, where the plaintiff, who had laid out large sums of money on the estate of the defendant's wife during her infancy, was not allowed to recover on an express promise made by the defendant after marriage, to indemnify the plaintiff for debts incurred by him in respect thereof, is conclusive upon the point. And the decision was soon afterwards followed in *Beaumont v. Reeve*[4], where the declaration alleged that the defendant had seduced the plaintiff and deprived her of the means of obtaining an honest livelihood, and had, when breaking off the connection, promised to pay her an annuity. The consideration was not illegal, and money actually paid in pursuance of the promise could not have been recovered. But it was merely " moral," and could not, therefore, support a simple contract. Mr Justice Patteson said " The seduction could give the plaintiff no direct right of action, and can, therefore, create no liability of any kind from which a consideration can arise[5]." And Mr Justice Coleridge added—" *Eastwood v. Kenyon* ...has established the principle that a moral consideration will not support an assumpsit[6]." The cases in which the " morality" of the situation arose from

[1] 2 East, 506.

[2] See these cases elaborately discussed in the note to *Wennall v. Adney* in 3 Bos. and Pull. p. 249. It is noteworthy, however, that the learned editors, writing in 1826, treat the doctrine as modern.

[3] 11 A. and E. 438.

[4] 8 Q. B. 483.

[5] 8 Q. B. at p. 487.

[6] 8 Q. B. at p. 487.

the fact that the defendant, though at the time of making the promise under no liability, had previously been under a legal liability which he then professed to revive, will be dealt with under the head of "past" considerations, to which we may now turn.

It has long been settled that the mere existence of a past benefit conferred spontaneously on the defendant by the plaintiff, or a detriment voluntarily undergone by the plaintiff on behalf of the defendant, will not support a subsequent parol promise by the latter. In the old case of *Hunt v. Bate*[1], decided in 1658, the defendant had voluntarily become surety for the plaintiff's servant, during the absence and in the ignorance of the plaintiff. The latter subsequently promised to hold the defendant harmless, but the promise was decided to be unenforceable, on the ground of want of consideration. This decision, which has since been followed in several cases[2], and has never of late years been questioned, lays down clearly the general rule, that a past consideration will not support a subsequent parol promise.

But to this rule many exceptions are alleged. In the first place, it is undoubtedly law that a subsequent promise (now required by statute to be in writing) to pay a debt barred by a Statute of Limitations is valid without other consideration than the existence of the previous debt[3]. And,

[1] Dyer, 272, *a*.

[2] *Hayes v. Warren*, 2 Str. 932. *Roscorla v. Thomas* 3 Q. B. 324. The decisions quoted in Smith's Leading Cases (9th ed.) I. p. 159 do not, in many instances, appear to deal with the point.

[3] *Holmes v. Mackrell*, 3 C. B., N. S. 789. The statutes in question are—9 Geo. IV. c. 14, requiring the subsequent promise to be

until recently, similar rules prevailed with regard to
promises to discharge debts incurred during infancy[1],
or previous to bankruptcy[2]. The two latter classes
of cases have been abolished by statute[3], and it has
been suggested that, in the former, the promise to
pay only amounts to a waiver of a procedural rule.
But the writer's reasons for regarding this explanation
as insufficient have been given elsewhere[4]; and he
deems it better to class the cases of revival of barred
debts as real exceptions to the general rule against
the sufficiency of past considerations.

The next exception is founded upon the well-
known decision of *Lampleigh v. Brathwait*[5], where
it was laid down, that if the past consideration had
been induced by the defendant's request, it would
support the new promise. The case of *Lampleigh v.
Brathwait* was decided in 1615. The defendant had
requested the plaintiff to procure for him a pardon
from the king, and, after the plaintiff had so endeavoured, had promised to give him £100 for his pains.
Now, apart from questions of public policy, which
were not argued in the case[6], it is clear that if the
defendant had originally said to the plaintiff—" Do

in writing, and 19 and 20 Vic. c. 97, allowing it to be signed by an
agent.

[1] *Cohen v. Armstrong*, 1 M. and S. 724.

[2] *Lobb v. Stanley*, 5 Q. B. 574; *Trueman v. Fenton*, 2 Cowp.
544.

[3] 37 and 38 Vic. c. 62 (infancy), 46 and 47 Vic. c. 52, § 30 (2).

[4] ante p. 16.   [5] Hobart, 105.

[6] There is strong reason for supposing that the consideration
would now be held bad on the ground of impolicy. *Norman v.
Cole*, 3 Esp. 253.

your endeavour, and I will give you £100"—he would have been liable. Therefore, the whole fault of the endeavour, as a consideration, lay in the fact that it had been done before the promise was given.

The case of *Lampleigh v. Brathwait* is noticeable on several grounds. In the first place, it emphatically repudiated the doctrine that the mere existence of a past consideration, not moved by the defendant's request, will support a simple promise. "It was agreed" said the learned Chief Justice who reported the case, "that a mere voluntary courtesy will not have consideration to support an assumpsit[1]." So that a past consideration of itself is not sufficient[2].

Moreover, the main object of the defendant appears to have been to disprove the genuineness of the services rendered by the plaintiff, and he did not take the objection to the consideration until the jury had given a verdict for the plaintiff. Then he moved in arrest of judgment, alleging that the consideration was past; but by this time the contract was on record, and the judges were naturally indisposed to upset it on a technical ground.

Thirdly, it will be noted, in reading the report, that the judges who constituted the Court were divided in opinion; and, though the difference apparently arose on the main contention of the defendant, and not on the argument with respect to

[1] Hobart, 106.

[2] This doctrine has of course been followed in cases to the decision of which it was actually necessary. e.g. *Roscorla v. Thomas* 3 Q. B. 234.

the consideration, yet its existence cannot be entirely overlooked.

Finally, it is worth serious reflection that, as has been pointed out by Sir William Anson[1], the decision in *Lampleigh v. Brathwait* has not received the direct support of any recent authority except one Irish case, that of *Bradford v. Roulston*[2], decided in 1858. On the other hand, in a comparatively recent and very important case[3], Chief Justice Erle endeavoured to explain it away by suggesting that the true relation of the express promise to the consideration is in the nature of evidence to fix the damages for breach of an implied promise arising therefrom.

But it is submitted that the judgment of the Irish Chief Baron in *Bradford v. Roulston*[4], and the conduct of the Court in *Wilkinson v. Oliveira*[5], though not sufficient to tie the hands of English judges, must have very great weight as indirect expressions of opinion. In the former case the learned Chief Baron most elaborately reviewed the decisions, and although (as Sir W. Anson points out)[6] he does not appear to have noticed the scantiness of recent authority, he did undoubtedly notice the disparaging *dicta* which had been uttered with respect to the rule laid down in *Lampleigh v. Brathwait*, and, in spite of these *dicta*, he decided to follow that rule. " I cannot," he says[7], " in deference to those expressions of opinion, pronounce a judgment reversing a series

---

[1] at p. 93.   [2] 8 Ir. C. L. 468.
[3] *Kennedy v. Broun*, 13 C. B., N. S. 677.
[4] 8 Ir. C. L. R. 468.   [5] 1 Bing. N. C. 490.
[6] at p. 95.   [7] 8 Ir. C. L. R. at p. 482.

of decisions made by successive judges, and establishing a rule of law that has been understood to prevail for, certainly, more than two centuries." And although the case of *Wilkinson v. Oliveira*[1] is certainly not in words a direct authority for the rule, it approaches as nearly to that position as can well be imagined. In that case, the plaintiff alleged that he, at the request of the defendant, "gave" the latter a document which proved of great value to him, and was, in fact, the means of his recovering a large sum of money, and that *thereupon* the defendant promised to give the plaintiff £1000 in consideration thereof. The defendant's counsel relied almost entirely on the use of the word "gave" in the declaration, and the Court, in pronouncing judgment for the plaintiff, did not deem it necessary to refer to the "past" character of the consideration, evidently assuming that to be no objection. It seems then too much to say that the rule in *Lampleigh v. Brathwait* is not law.

Further, it has been held that the request, by which the consideration is supposed to have been moved, may be implied, if the circumstances warrant the implication. It is said that an adoption of the benefits conferred by such consideration will raise a presumption that it was moved by the defendant's request. Thus, in the case of *Barber v. Brown*[2], the defendant had paid the ground rents of certain leasehold property which the plaintiff claimed, and which, in fact, belonged to him, though for some

---

[1] 1 Bing. N. C. 490.   [2] 1 C. B., N. S. 121.

time he had been in ignorance of his rights. The defendant was allowed to set off the payments of ground rent, on the principle that the plaintiff had reaped the advantage of them in the preservation of the leaseholds, and that the law would imply a request by him to make the payments. It is true that in this case the promise to repay was implied as well as the request, but the learned judge expressly said, " We are therefore entitled to say that this money was paid at the request of the plaintiff and must be allowed by way of set-off[1]." The same rule had been previously applied to a substantive action in the case of *Pawle v. Gunn*[2].

A request will also, it is said, be implied in cases where the plaintiff has voluntarily done what the defendant was legally compellable to do, and the defendant has subsequently made an express promise in consideration thereof. Thus, where the plaintiff had attended, as medical adviser, a pauper for whom the defendant was bound to provide, and the defendant subsequently used language which the court held to amount to a promise to pay, it was ruled that the previous request might be implied[3]. In an earlier case it had been decided that, where there was no evidence of an actual promise by the parish of settlement to repay monies expended on a pauper by the parish of residence, such a promise would *not* be implied from the legal liability of the parish of

---

[1] 1 C. B., N. S. at p. 151.
[2] 4 Bing. N. C. 445.
[3] *Wing v. Mill*, 1 B. and Ald. 104, (1817).

settlement[1]. And this case is sometimes[2] quoted as an authority for the doctrine that, although the law will in cases of voluntary considerations imply the request, it will not imply the subsequent promise. This view is, no doubt, supported, to a certain extent, by the words of Lord Ellenborough[3], but Mr Justice Le Blanc shews that other arguments influenced the Court, for he insists that the plaintiff, no less than the defendant parish, was bound to maintain the pauper during his illness. And in the later case of *Paynter v. Williams*[4], which, like *Wing v. Mill*, was for a parish doctor's bill, the evidence barely raised the presumption of an actual promise. The plaintiff had, in fact, sent the defendant a letter, which was not produced at the trial, and of the contents of which no evidence was given; and the defendant had thereupon renewed the pauper's allowance, which had been discontinued. There was no other communication between plaintiff and defendant. It is hard to see how such a promise can be called express.

A wider objection to the whole theory, of implied requests arising out of voluntary performances by one person of the legal duty of another, has been taken by Sir William Anson, who considers that " the cases cited in support of it seem to fail, on examination, to bear it out.[5]" But this is too sweeping. Doubtless the cases are nearly all upon one class of facts, a circumstance which, perhaps, narrows their

---

[1] *Atkins v. Banwell*, 2 East, 505.
[2] e.g. by Smith. *Leading Cases*, (9th ed.) i. p. 160.
[3] 2 East, at p. 506.   [4] 1 C. and M. 810.   [5] p. 99.

efficacy as declarations of principle. Doubtless, moreover, none of them are very recent; that of *Paynter v. Williams*[1], decided in 1833, being the most modern. But, on the other hand, the arguments and the judgments are based on general principles. In the latest case, Baron Bayley expressly disclaims a view which has been put forward to explain the cases—that the plaintiff really acted as the defendant's agent of necessity—saying, " The legal liability is not alone sufficient to enable the party to maintain the action, without a retainer *or adoption* of the plaintiff on the part of the parish. The legal liability of the parish does not give anyone who chooses to attend a pauper and supply him with medicines a right to call on them for payment[2]." The general principle is also stated in the meagre reports of *Watson v. Turner*[3], though the previous duty of the defendant is there placed only on a moral basis, which makes the rule still stronger.

But there is, undoubtedly, one class of cases in which, not merely the previous request, but also the subsequent promise, will be implied. If, as between plaintiff and defendant, the defendant is primarily liable to perform a certain duty, and the plaintiff performs that duty under some compulsion of law, he will be allowed to recover compensation from the defendant. Thus, if the transferee of shares in a company does not pay future calls, and the transferor is made liable in the course of winding-up proceed-

[1] 1 C. and M. 810.   [2] 1 C. and M. at p. 819.
[3] Buller's N. P. 147 *n.*

ings, he can recover the amount he is compelled to pay from the transferee, the latter being the person primarily responsible[1]. If an original lessee is called upon by the lessor to make good breaches of covenant committed by an assignee to whom he has transferred the lease, he will be entitled to compensation from the assignee[2]. And this, apparently, whether there is or is not any express covenant in existence between plaintiff and defendant. In the case of *Moule v. Garrett*, Chief Justice Cockburn said:— "Where one person is compelled to pay damages by the legal default of another, he is entitled to recover from the person by whose default the damage was occasioned the sum so paid[3]."

This clear and unequivocal statement of the principle prompts the suggestion that it might be advantageous to drop the elaborate fiction of an implied request and implied promise altogether, and base the rule on the simple doctrine of law. Doubtless, when it was necessary for a plaintiff to bring his claim within a particular form of action, and no nearer form presented itself, for cases such as we have specified, than the action of *assumpsit*, it was necessary to allege a promise in order to bring the case within the form, and an antecedent request to avoid the operation of the doctrine laid down in *Hunt v. Bate*[4]. The origin of the fictions is clear. But forms of actions are now abolished; and it would

---

[1] *Roberts v. Crowe*, L. R. 7 C. P. 629. *Kellock v. Enthoven*, L. R. 9 Q. B. 241.

[2] *Moule v. Garrett*, L. R. 7 Exch. 101.   [3] *ib.* at p. 104.

[4] ante p. 60.

seem better to state the rule in its simplest way, as a principle of law applicable to a particular state of circumstances[1].

Before leaving the subject, however, it may be well to call attention to the very definite limits of the rule. The plaintiff has only a right to recover "when he has been compelled to pay by the legal default of another," i.e. when the defendant's default is the real cause of his expenditure. If he has voluntarily undertaken the expense, or has incurred it through his own act or default, he has no claim. Thus, where the indorser of a bill of exchange, upon failure of payment by the acceptor, paid part of the amount due to the holder, before he had received notice of dishonour, and therefore, when he was not bound to make the payment, he was held not entitled to recover the amount from the acceptor[2]. And where the plaintiff had seized the defendant's furniture under a bill of sale, and, instead of removing it, left it on the defendant's premises, where it was distrained for rent, and the plaintiff paid the rent to save his furniture, he was defeated in an attempt to recover the amount from the defendant[3]. This was the case of *England v. Marsden*[4], and though

---

[1] As to the manner in which these cases came within the scope of *assumpsit*, cf. Professor Ames, *Harvard Law Review*, 1888, p. 60.

[2] *Sleigh v. Sleigh.* 5 Exch. 514.

[3] Presumably the decision would have been otherwise if there had been an express covenant in the bill of sale for payment of rent.

[4] L. R. 1 C. P. 529.

that case has been commented upon rather unfavourably more than once[1], it is still law.

Moreover, it has been held that a consideration from which the law implies a promise will not support any other promise than that implied by the law, even though such other promise be made in express terms. In *Hopkins v. Logan*[2] the plaintiff sued upon a promise by the defendant to pay *at a future date* a balance found to be due from him on account stated. A declaration on the account would have been good, for the law implies a promise to pay the balance of an account. But the Court of Exchequer held that there was no consideration to support an express promise differing from that implied by law, even though the difference was for the defendant's benefit. In *Kaye v. Dutton*[3] it was suggested by Chief Justice Tindal, that where the consideration was one from which the law could imply *no* promise, it might support any express promise otherwise unobjectionable. But the effect of the suggestion, if carried out, would practically be to upset the whole doctrine of *Hunt v. Bate*. The existence of the limit laid down by *Hopkins v. Logan* shews clearly the non-contractual character of the implied request and promise.

Hitherto we have considered those classes of cases in which the consideration, though apparently genuine, is (with some few exceptions) really delusive. We have now to advert to the examples in which an

---

[1] e.g. in *ex parte Bishop*, 15 Ch. D. at p. 417, and *Edmunds v. Wallingford*, 14 Q. B. D. at 816.

[2] 5 M. and W. 241.   [3] 8 Scott N. R. at p. 502.

apparently unreal consideration has been held to be genuine.

One of the most obvious of these is the case in which *B* undertakes to do something, without reward, in connection with the goods of *A*, which are thereupon delivered into his custody. It has been undoubted law, ever since the decision in *Coggs v. Bernard*[1], that if by the negligence of *B* or his servants the goods are damaged, *B* is responsible. Now these transactions may be looked at in two lights, either as *bailments* transferring *jura in rem* from *A* to *B*, and entitling *A* to claim return of the subject matter in certain cases, or as contracts, creating *jura in personam*, of *A* against *B*, and *B* against *A*. It is usual for English writers to confuse these two aspects in the hybrid term "contract of bailment," but it is submitted that a bailment is not a contract, though it may have a contract annexed to it. And this, notwithstanding that *jura in rem* cannot now be directly recovered by any process known to English law.

With the rights of *A* as bailor or owner, we shall not speak here. They will fall under that part of the chapter which deals with conveyances. We will speak here only of his rights arising from the contract annexed to the bailment.

It was urged in *Coggs v. Bernard* that the plaintiff could not recover upon the defendant's promise, because there was no consideration for it. But, in dealing with this objection, Lord Holt said,

---

[1] Ld. Raymond, 909.

"To this I answer that the owner's trusting him with the goods is a sufficient consideration to oblige him to a careful management." The limits of Lord Holt's words are obvious; the defendant is only liable in case of *negligence*, and as the declaration in *Coggs v. Bernard* alleged negligence, there was in strictness no necessity to enquire whether the defendant would have been bound absolutely to fulfil his promise. But it would seem, on general principles, that if the consideration were genuine, he would be so liable[1]. And Lord Holt gave it as his opinion that the mere delivery of goods to a man would be sufficient consideration for his promise to return them. The difficulty arises where the promise is implied, not express, and the question is whether the bailee is bound as an insurer who absolutely guarantees the safety of the goods, or as a person who merely promises to take due care. But questions of this kind depend very much upon the general circumstances of the case. With regard to our special point, it is now settled and clear, that the risk which the plaintiff runs in parting with his goods is sufficient detriment to him to constitute a genuine consideration[2].

Another example of consideration, apparently unreal but held to be genuine, is that established by the decisions in *Shadwell v. Shadwell*[3] and *Scotson v. Pegg*[4], where the plaintiff, being under a liability to a third person to perform a certain act, agreed with

[1] *Paradine v. Jane*, Aleyn, 26.
[2] *Bainbridge v. Firmstone* 8 A. and E. 743.
[3] 9 C. B., N. S. 159.   [4] 6 H. and N. 295.

the defendant to perform and did perform the same act, and the promise was held genuine consideration for a counter promise by the defendant. The principle of these decisions and the probable effect on them of recent legislation have been previously discussed[1].

Finally, as an example of a genuine, though apparently unreal consideration, we may notice the abandonment of a really unsupportable but *bonâ fide* claim. The cases have now put the matter on a fairly distinct footing. For a long time it had been admitted that, when legal proceedings had actually been commenced, the abandonment by one party of further proceedings was a sufficient consideration to support a promise by the other[2]. But in the year 1861 the principle was extended to cover a case in which no actual proceedings had been commenced. In *Cook v. Wright*[3] the plaintiffs, official persons, had alleged the liability of the defendant to pay the cost of certain repairs executed by them. The defendant denied his liability. And, as a matter of law, he was right. But the plaintiffs, *bonâ fide* believing in the legality of their claim, threatened to enforce it, and thereupon, in consideration of their withdrawing it, the defendants gave them certain promissory notes. It was held that there was genuine consideration for the notes.

Nine years later, this decision was fully adopted

---

[1] ante p. 21.

[2] *Longridge v. Dorville*, 5 B. and Ald. 117. *Atlee v. Backhouse*, 3 M. and W. 633.

[3] 1 B. and S. 559.

by the Court of Queen's Bench in the case of
Callister v. Bischoffscheim[1], when the plaintiff's
claim was not against the defendant, but against
third parties for whom the defendant acted.

But the other side of the rule is shewn in the
very recent decision in *Miles v. The New Zealand
Alford Estate Co.*[2], in which one of the defendants
had given a guarantee, in apprehension of a claim
being made against him, and to allay the angry
feelings of the shareholders. It was held that there
was no consideration for the guarantee, because in
fact the parties to whom it was given had not made
any claim, and, therefore, they had not abandoned
anything. Lord Justice Cotton observed: "In my
opinion to make a good consideration for this
contract, it must be shewn that there was something
which would bind the company not to institute
proceedings, and shewn also that in fact proceedings
were intended on behalf of the company[3]."

It must be noticed also that the rule turns
entirely on the *bona fides* of the claimant. The
abandonment of a claim which the claimant knows
to be groundless is no consideration. On the other
hand, the mere asserting of such a claim is, to use
the words of Chief Justice Tindal, almost *contra
bonos mores*[4]. And where the claim is manifestly
unfounded, the abandonment will not be a considera-

---

[1] L. R. 5 Q. B. 449.

[2] 32 Ch. D. 266.   [3] 32 Ch. D. at p. 285.

[4] *Wade v. Simeon*, 2 C. B. at p. 564, and expressions in *Callister v. Bischoffscheim* and *Cook v. Wright*.

tion, even though *both* parties believed in its validity[1].

10. *If* **executed**, *the consideration must not be an illegal or an immoral act, nor, if* **executory**, *must it contemplate an illegal or immoral object.*

Taking this last part of the canon first, it is clearly laid down in the cases, that an executory consideration which contemplates an illegal or immoral object, will not only be insufficient to support a parol promise, but will even vitiate a specialty contract. In the leading case of *Collins v. Blantern*[2], a bond was given to induce a prosecutor to withdraw from an indictment for felonious perjury. No mention of the consideration was made in the bond, and the plaintiff contended that no external evidence of it could be given. But the Court held that, though the existence of a consideration was unnecessary to support a bond, the existence of an illegal consideration rendered it void. And the Court also expressly disavowed the distinction which had formerly been taken between acts prohibited by statute and those forbidden by the common law.

It is equally clear, that if the consideration for a specialty be the promise or expectation of an immoral act, the consideration will vitiate the contract. Bonds given to ensure future irregular cohabitation have been constantly held void[3]. A

---

[1] *Jones v. Ashburnham*, 4 East, 455.

[2] 2 Wilson, 341.

[3] *Walker v. Perkins*, 1 W. Bl. 516. *Gray v. Mathias*, 5 Vesey J. 286.

fortiori, a consideration which contemplates an immorality will not support a simple contract.

It is equally clear that an executed consideration which consists of an illegal or an immoral act will not be a sufficient consideration. Thus, in the case of *Pearce v. Brooks*[1], the plaintiffs supplied goods to the defendant to be used (to their knowledge) for an immoral purpose, and they were not allowed to recover the price.

And, although a promise under seal does not require any consideration at all, it seems to be the law (though the matter is not wholly free from doubt) that if a specialty promise be given for an act executed, which act was illegal, the previous illegality will make the promise void. This was decided in 1854 by the Exchequer Chamber in the case of *Fisher v. Bridges*[2], which was an action on a covenant to pay the balance of purchase money due on a sale of land for an illegal purpose. The Court distinguished between the cases of immoral and illegal consideration, admitting, as is abundantly clear from decisions[3], that a merely immoral consideration, if executed, does not avoid a specialty promise.

11. *And the existence of an illegal or immoral consideration may be proved by external evidence, though the contract be embodied in writing, or even in a deed.*

---

[1] L. R. 1 Exch. 213, and in *Bennington v. Wallis*, 4 B. and A. 653.

[2] 3 E. and B. 642.

[3] e.g. *Marchioness of Annandale v. Harris*, 2 P. Wms. 432. *Nye v. Moseley*, 6 B. and C. 133.

This is also clear from the cases. In the leading decision of *Collins v. Blantern*[1], Chief Justice Wilmot allowed the illegal consideration to be pleaded, though the bond bore no mention of it; and although from his language we may perhaps infer that the common law courts had before his time hesitated to break in upon the general rule of evidence, it is clear that the Court of Chancery had no such scruples. And since the decision in *Collins v. Blantern* there has been no doubt about the common law doctrine[2]. *A fortiori,* an illegal or immoral consideration may be orally proved when the contract is only in writing[3].

12. *In the case of executory considerations which fail or become impossible, the promisor will be wholly or partially released from his obligation, and may even recover back money paid under the contract.*

In the case of *Chanter v. Leese*[4], the plaintiff, the owner of certain patent rights, sought to recover a sum of money which the defendants had agreed to pay for use of them. The defendants pleaded that the patents were invalid. Thereupon the plaintiff demurred to the plea. But judgment was given for the defendants, Lord Abinger saying[5], "If a man contract to pay a sum of money, in consideration that another has contracted to do certain things on

[1] 2 Wils. at p. 351.

[2] *Paxton v. Popham*, 9 East, 407. The rule is followed under the new practice. *Sound v. Grimwade*, 39 Ch. D. 605.

[3] *Williams v. Jones*, 5 B. and C. 108. *Rex v. Northwingfield*, 1 B. and Ad. 912. *Abbott v. Hendricks*, 1 M. and Gr. 791.

[4] 4 M. and W. 295.   [5] at p. 311.

his part, and it should turn out, before anything was done under it, that the latter was incapable of doing what he engaged to do, the contract is at an end." And it has been held that, where the promisor has, under such circumstances, paid any money under the contract, he can recover it as "money had and received." In the case of *Hudson v. Robinson*[1], the defendant had agreed to sell goods to the plaintiff, and the latter had paid for them. It subsequently appeared that the defendant could not make a title to the goods, and the plaintiff, who had received no benefit from the contract, sued to recover his purchase money. It was held that he was entitled to succeed. And where the defendant had agreed to grant the plaintiff a lease of certain premises, for which the plaintiff was to pay a premium, and, by a subsequent event, the granting of the lease became impossible, the plaintiff was allowed to recover all the money paid by him on account of the premium, although he had been let into possession of the premises and had occupied them for two years[2]. In this case the Court thought that the use and occupation formed no part of the consideration for which the premium was promised.

But where the consideration has been partly performed, it is the general doctrine that the failure of the remainder does not release the promisor, nor enable him to recover money paid, but only gives him the ordinary remedy for partial breach of contract. Thus, in the case of *Campbell v. Jones*[3],

[1] 4 M. and S. 475.   [2] *Wright v. Coles*, 8 C. B. 150.
[3] 6 T. R. 570.

the consideration for the defendant's covenant was the promise of the plaintiff to teach him a certain process, and to permit him to use a certain patent. When the plaintiff brought his action, the defendant demurred to the declaration, on the ground that it did not allege performance of the promise to teach. Judgment was, however, given for the plaintiff, Lord Ellenborough saying, "another ground on which the plaintiff is entitled to judgment is this, that the teaching of the defendant is not the *whole consideration* of the promise to pay." And in the recent case of *Bettini v. Gye*[1], the plaintiff was allowed to recover for breach of the defendant's promise to employ him as a singer, notwithstanding that he had partly failed to perform his own promise, which was the consideration for that of the defendant.

The rule is frequently stated by the judges in terms, which are, to a certain extent, misleading. It is said, for example, that the real test is whether the performance of the consideration was intended to be a " condition precedent" to the performance of the promise[2]. But here we run against the verbal difficulty before alluded to, that the consideration from one point of view is the promise from another. And so we may be compelled to say that promise and consideration are each precedent to the other ; which sounds absurd, reminding one of German officers at the door of a railway carriage. Nevertheless, this is very much what is attributed to Lord Mansfield, in

[1] 1 Q. B. D. 183. See also *Anglo-Egyptian Co. v. Rennie.* L. R. 10, C. P. 271.

[2] e.g. in *Bettini v. Gye* at p. 189.

the case of *Boone v. Eyre*[1], where his lordship is reported to have said—" The distinction is very clear, where mutual covenants go to the whole of the consideration on both sides, they are mutual conditions, *the one precedent to the other.*"

The true principle appears to be, that if I make a promise to *B*, in consideration of his counter-promise to me, I am not entitled to assume that *B* will not fulfil his promise, unless it proves to be wholly impossible for him to perform it, and, therefore, I must fulfil my promise, unless the terms of our agreement shew that my liability was not to begin until his promise was performed. And if a failure of consideration is only partial, the law declines to decide offhand how far that particular part in which failure occurs influenced my promise, leaving that to be determined in a separate proceeding. It has, however, been held, that where a definite and easily calculable part of the consideration has wholly failed, an action will lie to recover a proportionate part of money paid[2].

It is conceived that the modern rules on the subject of set-off and counter-claim, will, to some extent, at least, reduce the importance of this canon.

We have now concluded our outline of the present condition of the law upon the subject of

---

[1] Reported in 1 H. Bl. 273, (*n*).

[2] *Devaux v. Conolly*, 8 C. B. 640. Mr Justice Cresswell characterized the circumstances as " a simple case of failure of consideration." And see the language of Lindley, L. J. in *Mayor of Bootle v. Lancashire*, L. J. 60, Q. B. (N. S.) 327.

consideration in contract. Putting together the various canons which we have considered, we find that the net result is as follows.

Every true contract contains a promise. A consideration is a detriment or liability voluntarily incurred by the promisee [or a benefit conferred on the promisor at the instance of the promisee] in exchange for the promise. Such consideration may be either the performance, or the promise, of an act or forbearance. If it be the performance, the consideration is said to be *executed*, if the promise, to be *executory*. The existence of a consideration is essential to the validity of every simple contract, and, therefore, where by any rule of law an agreement must be reduced to writing as a condition precedent to becoming a contract, the consideration must appear in the writing, if in fact it was stated in the agreement. In certain cases, a consideration is essential also to the validity of a contract under seal, and, in nearly all cases, it is a condition precedent to the granting of the special remedy of "specific performance;" but in these cases the consideration need not be stated in the deed. In accordance with the general rule of law, the onus of proving the existence of a consideration usually rests upon the party setting up the contract, whether the consideration appears in writing or not. But, in the case of negotiable instruments, the existence of consideration is presumed, in the absence of suspicious circumstances. In ordinary cases it is immaterial whether or no the consideration be economically adequate to the promise, but gross inadequacy of consideration, though in itself no objection to the validity of a contract, either at law or in equity, may be evidence of fraud. On the other hand, the consideration must be genuine, and, if *executed*, it must not consist of an illegal or immoral act, nor, if *executory*, must it contemplate an illegal or immoral object; and the existence of an illegal or immoral consideration may be proved by external evidence, though the contract be embodied in writing, or even in a deed. Finally, in the case of executory considerations which fail or become impossible, the promisor will be wholly or partially released from his obligation, and may even recover back money paid under the contract.

B.

We now come to deal with the doctrine of consideration as it affects the subject of *conveyance*.

In the domain of conveyance the position of consideration is at once less important and less scientific than in that of contract. Broadly speaking, a conveyance does not require a consideration. It is only in certain cases that its presence is important, and these cases are not linked together by any general likeness which would enable them to be included in one scientific generalization. Consequently, the rules on the subject can only be stated vaguely; it will be necessary to refer to details rather as limitations than as examples. As the subject is small, we shall not treat the opinions of text-book writers separately from the genuine authorities.

1. *There are certain cases in which the existence*

of a consideration stamps the character of the transac-
tion, and annexes to it certain consequences.

For example, in the cases of bailment, or transfer
of possession, it is conceived that the existence of
consideration would go a long way towards determining the character of the transaction, and therewith,
of the liabilities of the respective parties. As has
been previously noticed[1], it is usual to speak of these
liabilities as arising from contract. But when the
parties are silent, the law practically annexes consequences to the circumstances of the bailment, which
is truly, at the present day, (whatever it may have
been in the days of the seisin of chattels) a conveyance
of a real right, the right of possession. And it can
hardly be contended that, in distinguishing the
various classes of bailments enumerated by Lord
Hale, the existence of consideration is not a fact of
the first importance.

But there is another and better case. It must
be taken now as settled law, since the case of
Cochrane v. Moore[2], that a *gift* of chattels, even
though *per verba de præsenti,* will not, if unaccom-
panied by delivery, pass the property in them. It
is equally clear that such a gift cannot be enforced
as an executory contract.

On the other hand, it appears to be the better
opinion[3] that on a *sale* of specific and completed

[1] ante p. 71.

[2] 25 Q. B. D. 57, disapproving *Winter v. Winter*, 4 L. T. N. S.
639, *Danby v. Tucker*, 31 W. R. 578, and *In re Ridgway*, 15 Q. B.
D. 447, and approving *Irons v. Smallpiece*, 2 B. and Ald. 551.

[3] Blackburn on *Sale* (2nd ed.), 242, Benjamin Part II. *Bailey*

chattels the property will pass without delivery, if such be the intention of the parties. It seems astounding that, at the present day, there should be any doubt about the law of such a common transaction. But, as a matter of fact, the point cannot be said to be entirely free from doubt, though unquestionably the balance of authority is in favour of the view that the property passes. If this view be correct, it can be but one thing which makes the difference between this case and the analogous case of gift, viz. the presence of consideration, which in fact decides the category to which the transaction shall belong. But, as the distinction, if it exists, was undoubtedly introduced many years ago, it will be better to postpone a discussion of its origin till we reach an earlier period.

Again, in the cases of " resulting trusts," the absence of a consideration is fruitful in important consequences. The doctrine of " resulting trusts," which has been copied from the older doctrine of " resulting uses[1]," proceeds broadly upon the presumption that, where the nominal grantee in a conveyance is obviously a volunteer as well as a

---

v. Culverwell, 2 M. and R. 564; implied in *Whitehouse v. Frost*, 12 East, 613, *Rugg v. Minett*, 11 East, 213, *Elliott v. Pybus*, 10 Bing. 512. *Rohde v. Thwaites*, 6 B. and C. 388. *White v. Wilks*, 5 Taunt. 175, *dictum* in *Cochrane v. Moore* at p. 73. *Contra*, Smith, *Mercantile Law* (10th ed.), 603. Blackstone (ed. 1766), II. 447. Williams, *Personal Property* (5th ed.), 37, *Tempest v. Fitzgerald*, 3 B. and Ald. 680, *Blenkinsop v. Clayton*, 7 Taunt. 596, *Goodale v. Skelton*, 2 H. Bl. 316.

[1] Per Lord Thurlow in *Fordyce v. Willis*, 3 Bro. C. C. at p. 586.

stranger, the real benefit of the transaction is intended to enure to the grantor or the party providing the consideration. There are two principal instances of the doctrine.

a. If a man convey property to a stranger in blood for no consideration, or for a nominal consideration, and there is nothing to shew that he intended him to take beneficially, there will be a resulting trust in favour of the grantor[1].

This doctrine was recently acted upon in the case of *Haigh v. Kaye*[2], where the plaintiff had conveyed an estate to the defendant, apparently for the consideration of £850, as stated in the deed, but really, as it was proved, for no consideration. The defendant was declared a trustee for the plaintiff, and the case is valuable as shewing that in these cases a party to the deed of conveyance may contradict its statements by external evidence. But, of course, the same liberty is given to the grantee of rebutting the implication of a resulting trust, by evidence which shews that the transaction was intended to be genuine. Thus, in the case of *Fowkes v. Pascoe*[3], an old lady had transferred stock previously standing in her own name alone, into the joint names of herself and a person who, though very intimate with her, was a stranger in blood, and towards whom the Court expressly decided she was not *in loco parentis*. After the lady's death her executors endeavoured to make the transferee, who

[1] Story, *Equity Jurisprudence* (13th English ed.), II. 531. Watson, *Compendium of Equity* (2nd ed.), 971.

[2] L. R. 7 Ch. 469.   [3] L. R. 10 Ch. 343.

had admittedly given nothing for the stock, a trustee for the estate. But the Court of Appeal, overruling the Master of the Rolls, admitted and acted upon parol evidence that the deceased had intended the transferee to take beneficially by survivorship. The same rule had been previously adopted in the case of *Benbow v. Townsend*[1].

It is, however, necessary to bear in mind one caution in dealing with this class of cases. Inasmuch as the whole equitable doctrine of trusts depends upon the iniquity of allowing the trustee to violate his conscience by keeping for himself that which he took for another, if it can be shewn that the grantee had, at the time of the grant, no knowledge of its existence, he cannot be charged upon an implied trust. In one case a Government pension was obtained for a married woman, and, to prevent any claims on it by her husband, from whom she was separated, it was taken in the name of a stranger, who in fact was ignorant of the whole transaction till long after its accomplishment[2]. It was held that he could not be made a trustee. Whether, in such case, the property in the grant would be vested in him at all, is another matter.

b. Where a conveyance is taken in the name of A, but B pays the purchase-money, A will be held a trustee for B[3].

This rule was laid down with unequivocal clearness by Chief Baron Hotham in the leading case of

---

[1] 1 Myl. and K. 506.
[2] *Fordyce v. Willis*, 3 Bro. C. C. 577.
[3] Story, II. 534. Watson, 969.

Dyer v. Dyer[1]. "The clear result of all the cases" said his lordship "without a single exception, is, that the trust of a legal estate, whether freehold, copyhold, or leasehold; whether taken in the names of the purchasers and others jointly, or in the names of others without that of the purchaser; whether in one name or several, whether jointly or *successive*, results to the man who advances the purchase-money[2]." As a matter of fact *Dyer's case* is not a direct authority for the rule itself, but for an exception from it which we shall immediately notice; but it proceeded on a clear admission of the general rule, and if any positive authority for that be needed, we may quote the decision in *Wray v. Steele*[3]. But really the doctrine has never been doubted since the anonymous case in 1684, quoted by Ventris[4].

As a general rule, the Statute of Frauds does not apply to resulting trusts, because they arise by implication of law, and are therefore expressly excluded from its operation[5]. But where the consideration for a conveyance is expressed to be paid by the grantee, the courts have refused to admit evidence, *after his death*, to shew that he did not really pay it, on the ground that such a course would defeat the intention of the statute[6]. It is, of course, different where the facts appear on the conveyance, and, where the grantee is alive, the courts

---

[1] 2 Cox, 92.   [2] 2 Cox at p. 93.
[3] 2 Vesey and B. 388.   [4] 2 Ventris, 361.
[5] 29 Car. II. c. 3, § 8.
[6] *Kirk v. Webb*, Ch. Prec. 84.   *Heron v. Heron*, *ibid.* 163. *Quære* if these cases are now law. (*Groves v. Groves*, 3 Y. and J. 163.)

have not hesitated to admit oral evidence to vary the deed.

But there is one very important point to be noticed on the whole doctrine of resulting trusts. Inasmuch as a resulting trust by no means arises from every voluntary conveyance[1], but only from those in which there is no other adequate explanation of the circumstances, it is the rule, that where the circumstances themselves rebut the implication, there will be no resulting trust. The most important example of this doctrine occurs where the person paying the consideration stands towards the nominal grantee *in loco parentis*. This was the actual point decided in *Dyer v. Dyer*[2], where a man had purchased copyholds in the names of himself, his wife, and his eldest son. Although the purchaser treated the property as his own, devising it by his will to his younger son, the plaintiff, it was held that the circumstances of the purchase sufficiently explained the transaction as an "advancement" to the eldest son during his father's lifetime, and that the father could not afterwards change his mind. This case, which appears to have been the origin of the rule in its present form, having overridden an earlier un- reported case of *Dickinson v. Shaw*, seems to lay it down that the presumption from relationship is absolute, or *juris et de jure*, incapable of being rebutted by evidence. The Chief Baron, commenting on previous decisions which treated the relationship

[1] *Young v. Peachy* 2 Atkyns, 256. *Lloyd v. Spillet, ibid.* 150.
[2] 2 Cox, 92.

as mere *evidence*, capable of being outweighed by counter-evidence, observed that such a construction would open the door to endless enquiries, and pretty clearly expressed his view that the relationship was really a valuable consideration which removed the transaction from the category of voluntary conveyances. " I think it would have been a more simple doctrine if the children had been considered as purchasers for a valuable consideration[1]." And, after reviewing some of the difficulties to which a contrary doctrine gave rise, the learned judge added —" Now if it were once laid down that the son was to be taken as a purchaser for valuable consideration, all these matters of presumption would be avoided[2]." And he finally came to the conclusion that "if it is meant to be a trust, the purchaser must shew that intention by a declaration of trust[3]."

The view taken by the Chief Baron in *Dyer v. Dyer* was supported, twenty years later, in *Finch v. Finch*[4], to the extent that Lord Eldon said—" Purchase is an advancement *prima facie*; and in this sense; that this principle of law and presumption is not to be frittered away by nice refinements[5]." And he held that the doctrine applied to the case of a reversion. This, then, seems to be now the law, that the relationship raises a strong presumption of advancement, but only a presumption, which may be rebutted by clear contemporary evidence[6]. The

---

[1] 2 Cox at p. 94.
[2] 2 Cox at p. 95.
[3] *ibid.* p. 98.
[4] 15 Vesey, 43 (1808).
[5] 15 Vesey at p. 50.
[6] *Stock v. McAvoy*, L. R. 15 Eq. 55.

relationship has been held to cover cases of husband and wife[1], father and illegitimate child[2], grandfather and grandchild[3], and mother and child[4].

In two classes of conveyances based upon the Statute of Uses, viz. the Bargain and Sale of lands, and the Covenant to stand seized, the presence of consideration was essential.   But, although these forms of conveyance are still technically possible, the passing of the 8 and 9 Vic. c. 106 has long rendered them practically obsolete; for as all estates, except estates tail, can now be disposed of by ordinary secret conveyance, there is no necessity to resort to the indirect methods of the Bargain and Sale and Covenant to stand seized.   We shall reserve these transactions, therefore, for a future chapter, and pass to our second rule.

2.   *There are certain cases in which the conveyance, though valid as against the grantor, can be set aside by other persons on proof of want of consideration.*

These cases are nearly all founded on express statute.   It will be a convenient plan therefore, to enumerate them under the heading of the statutes upon which they are respectively founded.

a.   In the first place, the 13 Eliz. c. 5 makes all conveyances of lands or chattels devised to defraud " creditors and others " void as against those who are

---

[1] *Back v. Andrew*, 2 Vern. 120.   *Low v. Carter*, 1 Beav. 426, expressions in *Glaister v. Hewer*, 8 Vesey at 198.

[2] *Beckford v. Beckford*, Lofft. 490 (doubtful).

[3] *Ebrand v. Dancer*, 2 Ch. Ca. 26 (but the father was dead.)

[4] *Sayre v. Hughes*, L. R. 5 Eq. 376 (widowed mother).? married woman.   *Todd v. Moorhouse*, L. R. 19 Eq. at p. 71.

or might be injured by them, but against them only. The statute, however, expressly provides that its provisions shall not apply to any conveyances made upon " good " consideration and *bonâ fide*, to persons not having any notice of the fraud.

With regard to the nature of the fraud which will bring a transaction within the statute, we have nothing specially to do. Suffice it to say that it may appear from express evidence, as where a person, being about to enter upon a hazardous business, makes a voluntary settlement of the bulk of his property with a view of placing it beyond the risk of creditors[1], or from indirect implication, as where a voluntary settlement leaves the settlor insolvent[2]. Nay, " if the debts of the creditor by whom the voluntary settlement is impeached existed at the date of the settlement, and it is shewn that the remedy of the creditor is defeated or delayed by the existence of the settlement, it is immaterial whether the debtor was or was not solvent after making the settlement[3]."

It is sufficient here to point out, that, however fraudulent may be the intention of the grantor, however great the loss to the creditors, if the grantee act *bonâ fide*, and give " good " (which has always been read to mean what in modern times is generally called " valuable[4]") consideration, he will be perfectly

[1] *Mackay v. Douglas*, L. R. 14 Eq. 106. *Ex parte Russell*, 19 Ch. D. 588.

[2] *Freeman v. Pope*, L. R. 5 Ch. 538.

[3] Lord Westbury in *Spirett v. Willows*, 3 De G. J. and S. at p. 302.

[4] Since *Twyne's Case*, 3 Rep. 81 *a*.

safe[1]. It should be observed however, that the statute requires both consideration *and* good faith[2].

b. The 27 Eliz. c. 4, provides that conveyances of *lands tenements or hereditaments*, fraudulently made to deceive past or future purchasers, shall be void against such purchasers as have or shall purchase for money or other good consideration any interest in the same lands, tenements, and hereditaments. It also provides that conveyances reserving a power of revocation to the grantor shall be void against subsequent purchasers for money or other good consideration (who bought before the power of revocation) as well as persons claiming under them. But nothing in the Act is to make void any purchase made for good consideration AND *bonâ fide*.

The 27 Eliz. c. 4, is peculiarly important for our purpose, for it has been held, in construing it, that *every* conveyance made without consideration is void as against a subsequent purchaser for value, even though he had notice of the voluntary conveyance. The full doctrine is very old; the first part of it dates from the commencement of the 17th century[3], and the latter from a still earlier date, being resolved by the Court in *Gooch's Case*[4], decided in 1590. Both parts

[1] Even though he purchase an interest reserved by the settlor under the voluntary settlement. *Halifax Joint Stock Banking Co. v. Gledhill.* [1891.] 1 Ch. 31.

[2] *Perry Herrick v. Attwood,* 2 De Gex and J. 21. *Clarke v. Palmer,* 21 Ch. D. 124. These cases were decided on the 27 Eliz. c. 4; but it would seem that the reasoning would apply to the earlier statute. And see *Twyne's Case,* 3 Rep. 81 *a.*

[3] See the cases reviewed by Lord Ellenborough in *Doe v. Manning,* 9 East, 59.   [4] 5 Rep. 60, *a.*

of the rule, but especially the latter, have been animadverted upon in strong terms by judges of eminence[1], but it would seem that they are unquestionably law.

Upon the subject of revocable conveyances, it is said by a learned writer[2] that the mere presence of an absolute power of revocation ("at his will and pleasure") is sufficient to make the conveyance fraudulent within the statute, even though there be consideration. It is true that so very few persons are willing to give consideration for a revocable conveyance, that one would naturally expect the amount of authority on the subject to be small: but even the cases quoted by the learned writer hardly seem to bear out his assertion.

The first case to which he alludes, that of *Buller v. Waterhouse*, is thrice reported[3], twice very badly, once very well. In the report in Jones, which is the best, it appears that an estate was settled by husband and wife in consideration of the future marriage of their son. The settlement contained a power to revoke the uses in favour of husband or wife, with the consent of certain persons. In pursuance of this power, but without the consent of those persons, the wife, after the death of the husband, sold to the defendant. It does not appear who the plaintiff was, unless the rector of a living which was part of the property sold by the wife. But the jury specially

---

[1] e.g. in *Doe v. Manning* at pp. 64 and 71. *Buckle v. Mitchell*, 18 Vesey, 100.

[2] May, *Voluntary Dispositions of Property* (2nd. ed.), 210.

[3] In 3 Keb. 751, Thos. Jones, 94. 2 Shower, 46.

found that if the settlement was held fraudulent the defendant ought to have judgment. And as the Court unanimously gave judgment for the plaintiff, we may presume that they upheld the settlement.

Hungerford v. Earle was a case heard before the Lords Commissioners of the Great Seal in 1692. It is also reported three times[1], and it appears that the plaintiff sought to set aside a conveyance made to trustees for payment of the settlor's debts, and, therefore, presumably, revocable by him[2]. The plaintiff was a creditor whose debt was incurred subsequent to the settlement, and, the debt being secured by bond, seems to have been considered as a purchaser. Lord Commissioner Hutchins thought the settlement bad; but the other two Commissioners differed from him, and the matter was sent to law, whence no report survives.

In *Cross v. Faustenditch*[3], a revocable conveyance was certainly set aside in favour of a subsequent lessee for value. But there the conveyance, though on a consideration of natural affection, sufficient to lead uses as against the grantor, was clearly voluntary in the ordinary acceptation of the term.

In *Tyre v. Littleton*[4], the plaintiff's husband had been tenant by heriot service to the defendant, but some years before his death he had made a feoffment on consideration of marriage, to his son, with a stipulation that the latter should redemise to him for forty years, if he (the feoffor) should so long live.

---

[1] 2 Vern. 261.   Freeman, 119.   1 Eq. Cases Abr. 148.
[2] Qu. though.   There were limitations in favour of children.
[3] Cro. Jac. 180.   [4] 2 Brownl. 187.

It was held that the feoffment was good against the defendant, and that the plaintiff's husband was not his tenant at the time of his death.

It is true that certain expressions in *Twyne's Case*[1] and *Tyre v. Littleton*[2] seem to favour Mr May's view, but it may be doubted if there is any direct authority for the point.

With regard to the nature of the consideration which will be sufficient to take a conveyance out of the operation of the statutes of Elizabeth, it may be laid down, generally, that it must be a consideration such as would support a simple contract. Our examination of such considerations will, therefore, be available to guide us. But in some respects the rule is laxer. Thus, for example, a past consideration is generally recognized as sufficient to prevent the conveyance being regarded as voluntary, at least if there were any pressure by the grantee[3]. And it would seem that a conveyance, originally voluntary, may subsequently be rendered unimpeachable by the grantee giving consideration without fraudulent intent[4]; which is one reason why a purchaser cannot be compelled to take a title which involves the

---

[1] 3 Rep. 82 *b*.

[2] 2 Brownl. 189. But Coke expressly says that the good consideration takes the feoffment out of the statute.

[3] *Belcher v. Prittie*, 10 Bing. 408. *Ex parte Hodgkin*, L. R. 20 Eq. 746. *Ex parte Field*, 13 Ch. D. 106 *n*. (These were decisions on Bankruptcy Acts, but the principles involved were the same). *Hale v. Alland*, 18 C. B. 527.

[4] *Prodgers v. Langham*, 1 Sid. 133, approved in *Johnson v. Legard*, Turn. and R. 294.

overriding of a voluntary settlement[1]. As a rule, the requirements of both the statutes of Elizabeth on the subject of conveyances are the same; but it has been held that, in an otherwise voluntary assignment of leaseholds, the legal liability to the rent and covenants which falls on the assignee is sufficient to make the assignment good as against subsequent purchasers under the 27 Eliz. c. 4[2], though not as against creditors under the 13 Eliz. c. 5[3]. A merely nominal consideration, such as five shillings, will not be sufficient[4], although the Court will not, generally speaking, enter into the adequacy of a consideration[5]. Where no consideration is mentioned in the conveyance, any consideration not inconsistent with the terms of the deed may be proved *aliunde*[6].

c. We may notice the 12th section of the Bills of Sale Act 1882[7], which provides that every bill of sale (i. e. conveyance of personal chattels intended to remain in the possession of the grantor) made or given in consideration of any sum under £30 shall be void. There does not appear to be any decision on the point, but, as the Act of 1882 is expressly declared not to apply to bills of sale given otherwise

---

[1] *Clarke v. Willott*, L. R. 7 Exch. 313.

[2] *Price v. Jenkins*, 5 Ch. D. 619.

[3] *Ridler v. Ridler*, 22 Ch. D. 74. The distinction had been taken earlier viz. in *Walker v. Burrows*, 1 Atk. at p. 94.

[4] *Walker v. Burrows*, 1 Atk. 93.

[5] *Bayspoole v. Collins*, L. R. 6 Ch. 228, (purchasers). *In re Johnson*, 20 Ch. D. at p. 397. But see *Strong v. Strong*, 18 Beav. 408, and other cases.

[6] *Bayspoole v. Collins*, L. R. 6 Ch. 228.

[7] 45 and 46 Vic. c. 43.

than by way of security for money[1], it is probable that a bill of sale, not being a security for money, might be given for a consideration of less amount or value than £30.

d. We have now to refer to certain very important provisions of the Bankruptcy Act 1883, which render voluntary conveyances impeachable by creditors in an insolvency. The policy of these sections is very old; it has been enforced ever since the beginning of the 17th century[2]. But the precise method of enforcement seems to have been introduced by the Act of 1869[3].

In its final shape, as contained in the Bankruptcy Act 1883, this policy provides that a settlement not being made before *and* in consideration of marriage, nor in favour of a purchaser or incumbrancer in good faith *and* for valuable consideration, nor a settlement in favour of the settlor's wife or children of property which has accrued to the settlor after marriage in right of his wife, shall be *ipso facto* void against the trustee in bankruptcy, if within two years after its date the settlor becomes bankrupt, and similarly void if the bankruptcy occurs within ten years, unless the parties claiming under it can prove that its execution did not leave the settlor insolvent, *and* that the interest of the settlor passed to the trustee of the settlement on the execution thereof[4].

Briefly put, the section renders void all voluntary

---

[1] 45 and 46 Vic. c. 43, § 3.

[2] See 13 Eliz. c. 7, § 7, and 1 Jac. I. c. 15, § 1.

[3] 32 and 33 Vic. c. 71, §§ 91, 92.

[4] 46 and 47 Vic. c. 52, sec. 47.

settlements made within two years before bankruptcy, and throws on persons claiming under
voluntary settlements made within ten years, the
onus of proving that they were neither fraudulent
under the 13 Eliz. c. 5, nor merely colourable. Of
course, but for this section, the *onus* of proving the
fraud would lie upon the party alleging it, and it is
presumed that the section does not help anyone but
a trustee in bankruptcy.

With regard to what constitutes a "settlement"
under the section, although the interpretation clause
provides that it shall include "any conveyance or
transfer of property[1]," it has been held that it will
not cover an out and out gift of money by a father to
his son, to be expended at once[2]. "The end and
purpose of the thing" said Cave, J., "must be a
settlement, that is, a disposition of property to be
held for the enjoyment of some person[3]." It has
further been decided, that, in calculating the solvency
of a settlor where the settlement is impeached after
two years, any beneficial interest reserved by the
bankrupt in the settled property must be reckoned
as assets belonging to him, it being available for
distribution among his creditors, and, therefore, not
comprised in the settlement[4]. In the latter case
the Court also expressed an opinion that the "interest of the settlor passed to the trustees of
the settlement on the execution thereof," notwith-

---

[1] 46 and 47 Vic. c. 52, sec. 47 subs. 3.

[2] *Re Player*, 15 Q. B. D. 682.   [3] 15 Q. B. D. at p. 687.

[4] *Re Lowndes*, 18 Q. B. D. 677.

standing the reservation of the life interest[1]. The two opinions appear a little inconsistent, but the Court dwelt a good deal on the hardship of the trustee's contention.

The next section of the Bankruptcy Act[2] makes void as against the trustee any preferential payment or security given to any creditor within three months previous to the presentation of the petition upon which the adjudication is made; but there is a special provision that the section shall not affect the rights of persons making title in good faith and for valuable consideration through or under a creditor of the bankrupt. And a third section enacts, generally, that the provisions of the Act, except those relating to executions and attachments, and the voluntary settlements and preferences before alluded to, shall not invalidate any conveyance by or dealing with the bankrupt for valuable consideration, provided that the parties to the transaction, other than the bankrupt, have no notice of an available act of bankruptcy committed by the latter, and that the transaction actually takes place before the date of the receiving order[3]. Under the protection of similar saving clauses, it has been held that a post-nuptial settlement made by a bankrupt on his children should stand, because it was made at

---

[1] 18 Q. B. D. at 681. But where the settlor merely announced his intention of settling shares, without actually binding himself to do so, and the shares were, in fact, not transferred till nine years later, it was held that the settlement dated from the transfer of the shares. *Re Ashcroft*, 19 Q. B. D. 186.

[2] § 48.   [3] § 49.

the request of his father, who, in consideration of the bankrupt's conveyance, included in the settlement property of his own[1].

We have now examined the principal cases in which the existence of a consideration renders unassailable a conveyance which would otherwise be liable to be set aside for various causes[2]. We come to the concluding rule.

3. *There are certain cases in which the nature of the consideration for a conveyance must be publicly notified.*

These cases need not detain us long. They occur principally in those transactions of which the law, for some reason or another, requires public notice to be given.

Thus, for example, the Merchant Shipping Act of 1854[3] requires that the transfer of any share in a registered ship, to any person qualified to be the owner of a British ship, shall be by registered bill of sale in the form provided by the Act[4], which form, when examined, turns out to include a statement of the consideration.

Similarly, the Bills of Sale Act 1882[5], slightly amending its predecessor[6], requires that every bill of sale shall truly set forth the consideration for which it was given, and as a copy of such bill of sale has to

---

[1] *Hance v. Harding*, 20 Q. B. D. 732.

[2] In the list might fairly be included the protection afforded to purchasers for valuable consideration by the Land Registry Acts of Middlesex (7 Anne, c. 20), and Yorkshire (47 and 48 Vic. c. 54).

[3] 17 and 18 Vic. c. 104, § 55.   [4] Sched. E.

[5] 45 and 46 Vic. c. 43, § 8.   [6] 41 and 42 Vic. c. 31.

be registered, it follows that the statement of the consideration becomes public. Moreover, it is expressly provided[1] that one of the particulars of which any person paying the search fee may take a note is the amount of the consideration. The Courts have construed the 8th section of the Act with great strictness, but the decisions on the point hardly affect questions of principle.

We are now in a position to make one or two general remarks upon the position of the doctrine of consideration at the present day.

First then, we observe that it is almost purely an economic doctrine. The older view, that a consideration might consist of the recognition of a moral duty, is practically dead. A consideration now means a valuable consideration.

The adoption of this view has had two important consequences. It has greatly simplified the ascertainment of consideration; for it is comparatively easy to discover when there has been an economic gain or loss, while it is often very hard to decide whether there is a moral duty. And it has rendered the doctrine much more popular in Courts of Justice; for there has long been a feeling in the minds of English judges, that, at least so far as their civil jurisdiction goes, their functions are economic, not moral or censorial.

Secondly, we may notice that, where a consideration is required, it is now regarded, not as evidence, but as an essential element of the transaction. It is

[1] 41 and 42 Vic. c. 31, § 16.

true that there still survives the anomalous distinction which allows a specialty contract to be enforced by an action for damages, although there is no consideration for it.   But the way in which the Courts have broken in upon this doctrine, by requiring consideration in some cases, notwithstanding the existence of a specialty, and allowing consideration to be proved *aliunde* in others, shows that even this anomaly is giving way, while the doctrine of *Wain v. Warlters* is express authority for the later view. It is true also that older decisions so far regarded absence of consideration as proof of *mala fides*, that they declared all voluntary conveyances fraudulent as against purchasers injured by them.   But this doctrine has been expressly disapproved by later judges, who have recognized that consideration is a substantial element in itself, not merely an evidence of *bona fides*.   The strong desire of a commercial community to protect ordinary commercial transactions has done much to strengthen this view.

The latter reflection brings us to the notion which has, after all, been the great advocate of the doctrine of consideration in modern times.

Some of the elements of contract are essential. No one can imagine legal tribunals enforcing a contract unless it was made between capable parties, and contemplated a definite and legal object agreed upon by those parties.   But at this point unanimity ceases.   Almost all systems of law, at some period or another, have seen that some other element must be present to justify the enforcement of the transaction. Except in a very advanced stage, no system of law will undertake to enforce all agreements made between capable parties and having definite and lawful objects. The Roman Law ultimately came very near this point, but never reached it. English law has never professed to adopt it.

The question is—What further element shall be required? And upon the answer to this question it depends whether or not the system answering it shall have a scientific or an empirical Law of Contract. The Roman law answered the question by saying—The further element shall consist of some one of a list of circumstances which are recognized as suitable *causæ*, or occasions for the establishment of contracts. But, as the affairs of mankind are continually developing new incidents, it resulted that the Roman list of *causæ* was always becoming antiquated; and there existed, from time to time, classes of agreements which the Roman judicial officials were anxious to enforce, but which the Roman law steadily refused to recognize *as contracts*. They were mere *pacta*, not *actionibus vestita*, and therefore *nuda*. They could be enforced in a partial way, but not by the full machinery of *actio*. Hence the Roman Law of Contract remained to the last anomalous and unscientific.

English law, brought face to face with the same problem, has answered it in a different way. English law has, like the Roman, felt the need of some element of probability, some guarantee that the parties really intend to stand by the consequences of their actions. This guarantee it finds, not in the character of the external circumstances surrounding the transaction, but in the presence of a definite feature which, to English minds, stamps the transaction itself with the character of a business engagement. This feature assumes various disguises, but its physiological structure is everywhere the same. It is *quid pro quo*, the return which the promisee gives for the engagement of the promisor. And, inasmuch as the notion of exchange is one of the most widely spread and generally recognized of human conceptions, it follows that the idea of consideration is found to be applicable with marvellous facility to almost every class of undertaking. Thus English law, in effect, broadly says—If capable parties agree on a definite and legal object, and the promisee gives an ascertainable return of some economic value for the promise which he gets, that is a contract. Doubtless in some cases English law dispenses with consideration, out of deference to tradition. Doubtless in some cases it requires something more than consideration. But these are special exceptions. The general rule is simple and scientific, and the moulders of English law are entitled to the credit of having solved a problem which baffled the Roman jurists of the classical period, the problem of providing a definition of contract sufficiently wide to include the broad stream of serious human dealing, and sufficiently strong to resist the intrusion of the flood-waters of caprice.

In the domain of conveyance the position of the doctrine is much less clear. It is admitted that, with rare exceptions, consideration is not required for the transfer of real rights. Putting aside the doubtful, though important case, of the sale of specific chattels of a value less than £10, a voluntary conveyance will, at any rate if accompanied by delivery, be sufficient to pass property where the intention is clear. The doctrine of consideration in conveyancing law seems used partly as a test of *bona fides*, and partly as a mercantile guarantee of protection, much as the old doctrine of the purchaser in market overt or at the staple was used for the protection of ordinary mercantile transactions.

CHAPTER II.

It is very difficult to divide the history of English
law into periods which really represent changes
of condition. It is quite impossible to draw any
hard and fast lines. The development of English
law has been so irregular and anomalous, now by
judicial decisions and again by statute, now in the
Common Law Courts and again in Chancery, that
any attempt to erect unyielding barriers of chron-
ology would be alike futile and misleading. All
that we can do is to draw broad and elastic
boundaries, which will easily give way when con-
venience demands it.

To begin with, at what date shall we fix the
commencement of modern law? Shall it be the
amalgamation of the Courts in 1875, the abolition
of forms of action in 1852, the sweeping away of
real actions in 1834? Or again, shall we take
some great and epoch-making judge, like Lord
Mansfield, and make his accession to the bench
the starting point of a new system? Or, once
more, shall we say that the publication of some
great work inaugurates the new period? We must
try to find a point which shall attract as many
influences as possible.

Roughly, very roughly, the accession of George III. will serve as such a point. It is true that the formal changes had not been made, were not yet to be made for almost half a century. But the causes were beginning to work. Lord Mansfield had ascended his judicial throne in 1756, to reign as unquestioned king for thirty years. In six years more Blackstone was to publish those famous commentaries, the substance of which he was even then delivering as Vinerian professor at All Souls'. In the hands of Vesey, Durnford and East, and Barnewall and his various co-editors, law-reporting was about to assume its modern systematic and impersonal form. And the long list of *Abridgements*, those curious relics of mediæval scholasticism, which run from Fitzherbert and Rastell to Comyn and Cruise, was drawing to a close. From the ashes of the Vinerian Abridgement had risen up the phœnix of the Vinerian professorship, bearing on his wings the substantial volumes of Blackstone's *Commentaries*.

There is less uncertainty in the choice of a commencement for the previous period. In the year 1536 the official Reports known as the Year Books ceased to be compiled; and, shortly before that date, the Abridgements of Statham and Fitzherbert, the forerunners of the great race of private commentators, had appeared. The coincidence of dates is something more than a coincidence. For the fervour of the Legal Renaissance was upon men, and though they at first confined themselves to the old scholastic methods of gloss and commentary, the more original works of Staunforde, Plowden, Coke, and Finch were soon to show that a new race had arisen.

To this period, then, from the close of the Year Books to the accession of George III., but with large liberty to digress as occasion shall give cause, our present chapter will be devoted. It may be called the Period of the Abridgements, for those solemn productions cover the whole of its length. But a more vital distinction marks it off from the condition of things at the present day. It is a *formulary* period, in which the success of the parties depends not more on the merits of their cases than upon the skill of their advisers in framing those cases according to technical rules of art. And so strictly were those rules drawn, so refined and exact their application, that the *formulæ* produced under them are really our best guides to the state of the law in the period. It is a case in which, to use Sir Henry Maine's phrase, substantive law is "secreted in the interstices of procedure." We must endeavour then to attempt some examination of these *formulæ*.

For centuries prior to the year 1833, all civil procedure, at least in the royal courts, had been classed under the two great heads of Real and Personal actions. All actions brought to recover the possession of land or the right to a freehold were real[1]; all others personal. This division is at least as old as Bracton[2], to whom, probably, we owe the perverse rule which refused to allow a real action for the recovery of a movable[3]; it is followed by the

[1] Of course the action of the lessee for years was not real until the invention of the *Quare ejecit*, long after Bracton's time, (cf. Hale, *History of the Common Law*, Runnington, 1794, p. 287.)

[2] Bk. iii. 3, § 1.

[3] I do not, of course, mean to suggest that Bracton was responsible for the introduction of the rule; he merely perpetuated

Mirror[1] (whatever may be the date of that compilation); it is repeated by Littleton when he says— "Et sachez, mon fitz, que est un de pluis honorables, et laudables et profitables choses en nostre ley, daver le science de bien pleder en accions realx et personelx[2];" it is admitted by Coke in his commentary on the same passage[3]; and it is recognized by the modern statute which swept away the greater part of the real actions[4].

Putting aside for the present the class of real actions, as well as those known as "mixed," a combination of the two principal classes which was probably brought in to follow the Roman classification, and which is valueless for scientific purposes, we will confine ourselves for the present to the personal actions. These again, both at the beginning and end of our period, were recognized as being subdivided into two classes, those founded on contract and those founded on tort[5]. But, though the classification was orthodox, we find, at least at the end of our period, that there was considerable difference of opinion as to its precise application[6].

the archaic doctrine, which, in effect, was—*cherchez le voleur*. But he might easily, by a little wise heterodoxy, have anticipated the Mercantile Law Amendment Act by six centuries.

[1] Cap. II. § 1. Horne's classification is, however, very dubious.

[2] Tenures, III. 9, fo. 534.   [3] First Inst. 302 *b*.

[4] 3 and 4 Will. IV. c. 27.

[5] Bracton, III. 3 § 1, who then subdivides *actiones ex maleficiis* into civil and criminal. Blackstone, III. 117.

[6] It must be remembered that although the Uniformity of Process Act (2 Will. IV. c. 39) simplified the forms of writs, it by no means did away with the necessity for naming a form of action. See the precedents of writs in the Schedule.

Thus, while it was generally admitted that Debt, Account, and Covenant were on contract, and Trespass, Case, and Replevin on tort, the classification of Detinue and Assumpsit was very uncertain. By some writers they are put under contract, by others under tort. It so happens that these two actions are specially connected with our subject.

Let us take first the example of Detinue. In a very recent case before the Court of Appeal[1], Lord Justice Bramwell, though he did not deem it necessary to decide the point, expressed a strong opinion that the old form of action in detinue was founded on tort[2]. Lord Justice Brett took precisely the opposite view[3]. The Common Law Procedure Act 1852[4] clearly puts it as on tort[5], the County Courts Act 1850[6], equally clearly, as on contract[7]. Chitty, with a good deal of hesitation, classes it amongst contracts[8], and, certainly, both he and Wentworth, in their precedents of pleading, most carefully abstain from any words which could raise the presumption of a tort[9]. The plaintiff "casually lost" the subject-matter, and the same "came to the hands and possession" of the defendant. The plea was "non detinet" simply, instead of "not guilty," as in trover; and, after the General Rules of 1833, this plea was construed to be a simple denial of the fact of detainer, not a slander

[1] *Bryant v. Herbert*, 3 C. P. D. 389.

[2] 3 C. P. D. at p. 391.   [3] *ib*. at p. 392.

[4] 15 and 16 Vic. c. 76.   [5] Sched. B. (29).

[6] 13 and 14 Vic. c. 61.   [7] § 11.

[8] *On Pleading* (ed. 1844), I. 110.

[9] Chitty, II. 429, III. 241. Wentworth, *System of Pleading*, VII. 635—7.

of the plaintiff's title[1]. But, seeing that as a matter
of law the defendant, had he parted with the subject-
matter to a person who was not the true owner,
would have been liable to the latter for a conversion,
he was entitled to put the plaintiff to proof of his title.

On the other hand, an author on Practice whose
work reached a ninth edition in the year 1828[2],
clearly makes detinue a tort, and Blackstone, though
with his usual want of definiteness, seems to incline
the same way[3]. Whom are we to believe?

The opinion of Lord Justice Bramwell in *Herbert
v. Bryant*[4] was avowedly founded on a decision of
the Court of Exchequer in *Clements v. Flight*[5], a
purely technical decision, which, however, is none
the worse on that account for our purpose. But
the judgment of the Court of Exchequer merely
decided that the detainer alleged by the declaration
in detinue was an adverse detainer, and that a plea
which set up a tender was bad as being argumenta-
tive. The Court nowhere said that the allegation
of adverse possession was an allegation of tort;
and the plaintiff in his declaration did not claim
that he was entitled to possession. It must be
admitted, however, that the slightly earlier case
of *Gledstane v. Hewitt*[6] supplies the deficiency, for
there Mr Justice Bayley said[7]—"The plaintiff must
make out that he was entitled to the delivery of the
article, and that the defendant wrongly detained it;

[1] Chitty, ii. 429.
[2] Tidd, i. 4.
[3] iii. 117, 150.
[4] 3 C. P. D. at p. 389.
[5] 16 M. and W. 42.
[6] 1 Cr. and J. 565.
[7] 1 Cr. and J. at p. 570.

and if he can do that, he has done all that is necessary to maintain his action.......The action of detinue is an action of wrong."

Now both these last decisions relied in their turn upon an old case of *Isaack v. Clark*, decided in 1614, and fully reported by Bulstrode[1]. It is a very interesting case, but it does not seem to warrant the use made of it in later times. The plaintiff sued in trover for a bag of money deposited with the defendant as pledge for the performance of an act which had not been performed when the action was brought. The defendant pleaded "not guilty," and the jury found the facts in a special verdict. The Court gave judgment for the defendant, on the ground that his mere refusal to deliver was not in itself a conversion.

It will be seen then that this case did not, *prima facie*, turn upon detinue at all. But the judges made some very interesting remarks about the latter form of action, contrasting it all through with the form of trover. And the passage upon which later judges have fastened, as warranting the assertion that detinue is founded on tort, occurs in the judgment of Haughton, J., who said[2]—"It is onely found that he did request him to deliver this Money, and he refused to do it, and so much is in every Action of Detinue, *contradixit & adhuc contradicit*, this is the point of the Action of Detinue, but this is not conversion." That is to say, in the opinion of the learned judge, the gist of the action

[1] II. 306.   [2] II. Bulstrode at p. 308.

of Detinue does not amount to the tort of Trespass (on the case). And yet, from this opinion, later judges have drawn the conclusion that it does amount to a tort of another kind! Coke's view in the same case was that denial is only *evidence* of a conversion to go to the jury, but that it is the very essence of Detinue[1].

Indirectly, there is very strong evidence that Detinue was not a tort. To begin with, it could always be joined in the same action with Debt[2], and to hold that a definite claim, which in old days would have been enforced by a *præcipe quod reddat*, could be united with a claim for damages (as all tortious claims were), which required a *si te fecerit securum*[3], would be very strange. Again, until the passing of the 3 and 4 Will. IV. c. 42, the defendant in an action of Detinue could generally wage his law, a fact which rendered the action very unpopular[4]. And yet Blackstone[5], following Coke[6], tells us that wager of law never lay for a tort, because it was impossible to presume that the defendant had satisfied unliquidated damages. It did not even lie on Assumpsit.

But if we carry our researches a little farther back we shall find still greater cause for surprise. In explaining the writ of Debt, Fitzherbert points out[7] that, where the action is brought to recover, not

---

[1] II. Bulstrode, 314. [2] Chitty, II. 249.
[3] See Sellon, *Practice* (1798), p. XLV.
[4] Blackstone, III. 151. Chitty, I. 139.
[5] III. 346. [6] Co. Litt. 295 *a*.
[7] *Natura Brevium*, 119 G.

money, but any other chattels, the form of the writ is in the *detinet* only, and not in the *debet* and *detinet;* and, though he elsewhere gives distinct forms for the writ of detinue[1], it will be found that they correspond almost word for word with those of Debt in the *detinet,* county court for county court, and Common Pleas for Common Pleas. One step more, and we come to the end of this path of enquiry. In the *Registrum Brevium* there is no separate writ of Detinue at all, but the claims of chattels are mixed up with the claims of money under the one title of *Debitum;* the distinction between *debet* and *detinet* being, however, carefully observed in the writ itself[2]. The same is the rule in the forms given in the *Statutum Walliæ*[3]. What is the explanation of the mystery ?

Three things seem fairly clear. First, that the writ of Detinue had at one time no existence independently of the writ of Debt. This is proved by the references to the Register and the *Statutum Walliæ,* by the fact that the circumstances of Detinue are included by Glanville under the head of Debt[4], and by the similarity of the procedure in both cases. Second, that the origin of the procedure was popular, not royal; that it is really the old Teutonic plaint with the suit and wager of law, which retained its original characteristics after having been drawn into the King's Courts by the writs of *justicies* and *quominus*[5].

---

[1] 138 B.   [2] Fo. 139 (ed. 1689).
[3] 12 Edw. I.   [4] Lib. x. c. 13.
[5] The writ of *justicies* was directed to the sheriff commanding him to hear the case, and it was asserted by the royalists that such

Third, that it was in truth a *real action*, which the feudal theories of the Norman lawyers would not allow them to call real, because it did not necessarily concern the freehold. The gist of the action of Debt, and its variation, Detinue, really was at first that the defendant had got into his hands something that belonged to the plaintiff. There is no important difference in Glanville between the writ of right for lands[1] and the writ of debt[2]. And, so late as the end of the sixteenth century, it was said that where there was an obligation to pay money at different dates, debt would not lie until the last had become due, for " the entire debt is to be recovered[3]." This fact was, doubtless, another cause of the ultimate unpopularity of the form of action ; but the objection was, apparently, removed by the 8 and 9 Will. III. c. II. sect. 8.

As then the Norman lawyers obstinately refused to recognize a real action to recover a chattel, it became necessary for them to find some other place for the action of debt. If it was a personal action, was it on contract or on tort ?

Where the claim was for money, the fungible character of the subject-matter offered an easy solution of the difficulty. It could not matter much

a writ was necessary as a preliminary to any plaint in the County Court above the value of forty shillings. The writ of *quominus* pretended that the plaintiff was prevented by the defendant's default from satisfying a debt due to the king, and thereupon summoned the defendant to appear in the King's Court.

[1] I. 6.   [2] x. 2.
[3] *Taylor v. Foster*, Cro. Eliz. 807 (1601).

to the plaintiff whether he got one set of coins, or another of equal value. And so the Courts would consider that the real relief sought was that the defendant should pay an equivalent of the amount received by him. Where the claim was on an actual loan, no doubt the defendant had promised to repay, and there would be every reason for holding him bound by his promise, when that promise was founded on a cash receipt.

A similar line of argument would be adopted where the claim for chattels arose originally out of a bailment, or, as Bracton would have said, *re.* In many cases the defendant doubtless had promised to return the goods; in others he would have been held to have done so.

But it should be observed that, although the promise might colour the action, no one pretended, in Glanville's time, for example, that a mere promise was sufficient to ground an action of debt[1]. The possession of the actual property of the plaintiff by the defendant was the true ground of the action.

How then when claims in debt and detinue really arose without anything from which a promise could be implied?

As to debt, we must leave the question till we deal with assumpsit; in the cases of detinue the courts were left with the option of still treating them as founded on contract, or, seizing upon the *injuste* of the writ, of shifting the ground to tort, or of

---

[1] Lib. x. 12. The plaintiff might go to the Courts Christian, but he could get no relief in the King's Courts. And yet Glanville distinctly classes "debts" as arising out of contracts, (x. pr.)

allowing either ground. As a matter of fact, they chose the last alternative. In a count for detinue, as Lord Coke observed in *Isaack v. Clark*[1], it was allowable to found either upon a bailment, or upon a mere possession by the plaintiff, followed by a refusal to give up. That is, the plaintiff may count in contract or in tort. In later times the bailment, like the loss in trover, became an untraversable fiction, and so the distinction was lost. It was then said that the mere refusal was the gist of the action; and that, of course, looked very much like tort, and the plea of "not guilty" was allowed[2]. But the resemblance of detinue to a real action was never lost sight of. In *Isaack v. Clark*, Dodderidge, J., said of detinue—"This action implies property in the plaintiff, and no other can have this action[3]"—which was not the case in trover, although Lord Mansfield has spoken of that as an action to try property[4]. The judgment in detinue was that the defendant should restore the goods *or* pay the value[5]. And Chitty describes it[6] as being the only form of action except replevin (another Saxon process) by which personal chattels could be recovered *in specie*.

The practical upshot of this enquiry is, that, all through the period now before us, judges and lawyers

---

[1] II. Bulstrode, 312. "The ancient form of the Count in detinue, is observable, where the same is upon a Bailment, and where it is upon a *devenerunt ad manus*."

[2] Noy, p. 56.   [3] II. Bulstrode, 308.

[4] *Hambly v. Trott*, 1 Cowp. 373. But his lordship admitted that trover was "in form a tort."

[5] *Peters v. Heyward*, Cro. Jac. 682.   [6] I. p. 135.

were familiar with a form of action which was,
actually in many cases, and nominally in many more,
founded on contract, but upon a contract wholly
informal, not sanctified by the guarantee of a
seal, and often merely implied from conduct. The
vital point of the whole subject was that the defendant *had* the property of the plaintiff; and
though this is not consideration in the modern
sense, it is something very near it. It will not
altogether account for *Coggs v. Bernard*, but it will
be a strong element in the forces which produce
that decision. It will be amply sufficient to account
for *Bainbridge v. Firmstone*.

We need not trouble ourselves to enquire into
the history of Covenant, which was a recognized
form of action in Glanville's day[1], and which, it is
generally admitted, had nothing to do with the
doctrine of consideration. If a man had put his seal
(or, in old days, even if some one else had put his
seal[2]) to a charter, he was bound by the solemnity of
the act. The rule which requires consideration in
some cases of specialty contracts is quite modern.

The third great influence in the history of
contract was the action on *assumpsit*, or, to put it
more exactly, the Action of Trespass on the Case
upon Assumpsit. But, before we can see how this
influence arose, we must take up the writ of Debt at
the place where we left it.

It seems unquestionable that the writ of Debt
at first only lay where the plaintiff had transferred

---

[1] Glanville, x. 12.   [2] *ib.*

money or chattels to the defendant in the presence
of witnesses. Careful provision for these witnesses
was in fact made by early law; but that is beyond
our present enquiry.

It seems also clear that, whether we are to
believe Glanville or not[1], the action of debt soon
grew beyond these narrow limits. At any rate, by
the beginning of our period, it was possible to use it
for almost every case in which a liquidated sum of
money or specific chattel was due. Fitzherbert puts
it thus. "A writ of debt properly lieth where a man
oweth another a certain sum of money by obligation,
or by bargain for a thing sold, or by contract, or
upon a loan made by the creditor to the debtor[2]."
And we see by the Abridgements, which were
probably accepted as good law in their day, though
they have since been accused of misrepresenting
their materials, that a very liberal use was made of
the writ of Debt. A marshal who allowed his
prisoner to escape was liable in Debt for the amount
which he owed the execution creditor[3]; a head
landlord had the action of Debt against his tenant's
assignee for his rent, though there was no privity
between them[4]; a creditor to whom liquidated
damages had been awarded in a real action could

[1] Book x. *passim*. Glanville seems very doubtful whether the
action of debt can be brought for anything but an actual loan of
money or goods. Yet he gives a form of writ against a surety.

[2] 119 G. This is practically the rule laid down in the (old)
Natura Brevium, Fo. 61, of which, however, Fitzherbert speaks
somewhat disrespectfully in his Preface.

[3] Brooke, *Abridgment*, Dette, 22.

[4] Brooke, *Abridgment*, Dette, 8.

sue the defendant for them in Debt[1]; an annuitant
similarly for arrears of an expired annuity[2]; and a
merchant for the balance of account stated[3]. And
Perkins, while denying that a *cestui que use* who
makes a lease by parol may distrain, adds "But
it is said that he may have an action of debt for
the rent against the lessee, *because it is but as a
contract*[4]."

In the examples given by Fitzherbert there are
two which deserve especial notice. One is very
curious, as illustrating the doctrine of merger at an
early date, "If a man make a contract to pay certain
money for a thing sought by him; now if he make
an obligation" (*semble* a bond) "for this money, the
contract is discharged and he will not have a writ of
debt on the contract[5]." The other is still more
interesting. "And a man shall have a writ of debt
against him who becomes pledge for another by his
promise to pay a certain sum &c., without any deed
for it," (*sans ascun fait de ceo*)[6]. And the cognate
writ *de plegiis acquietandis* is said to lie for the
surety who has been compelled to pay the debt,
against the principal debtor, "But there has been

<hr>

[1] Brooke, *Abridgment*, Dette, 33.

[2] Brooke, Dette, 145. Whilst the annuity was running he
would have the writ of annuity.

[3] Brooke, Dette, 12. This action would also lie against the
debtor's executor, because the debtor could not have waged his law,
(*ib.* 67). But the writ lay only in the *detinet*, (Fitz. 119 M).

[4] *Profitable Book*, § 692.

[5] 121 M.

[6] 122 K. The 9th (1794) ed. translates "without any writing
made thereof." But?

question if this writ lies without shewing specialty for it, and it seems reasonable that the writ will be upheld[1]," [because of the wording of Magna Carta].

Now it is always dangerous to draw general conclusions from the contract of suretyship, because it is one which early systems regard as standing on a very exceptional footing. But it does seem a fair inference from these extracts that in Fitz-herbert's day the difference between specialty or obligation on the one hand, and contract or parol promise on the other, was clearly recognized, and that there was some little doubt as to the validity of a parol contract, even when made for a definite liquidated sum.

Taking, however, the actions of Debt as a whole, the only feature common to them all seems to have been the fact that they were brought to recover liquidated sums or specific chattels.

The theory still evidently is that the defendant has by some means got the plaintiff's property, and Brooke even questions whether in an action of Debt for corn or other grain the plaintiff shall recover the thing itself, or the value[2]. Doubtless, when it came to actual litigation, the plaintiff might have been very seriously embarrassed if he could not prove his case in one of the established modes, and it will be noticed that the instances of Debt given in the Abridgements are nearly all cases in which there

---

[1] 137 C.

[2] *Abridgment*, Dette, 211. Hale (*Analysis*, § 41, speaks of recovering " the debt ITSELF and damages for non-payment ").

could not be much doubt as to the facts. The Marshal's liability for the escape, and the defendant's for the assessed damages were proved by record, the liability for rent by the fact of possession, the claims on the annuity and the account by the deed of grant and the certificate of the auditors. But the question of form seems rarely to have been raised. The one question is—Has the plaintiff a specific claim?

But, although the Courts would not entertain actions of Debt for unliquidated claims, they were perfectly familiar with forms of action to recover unliquidated damages. Granted that the original notion of damages was that of the fixed money value of the plaintiff's limb, and that this was only modified by the notion of a fine to the king for such torts as involved a breach of the peace, the more modern view of damages, as a pecuniary compensation specially assessed as the equivalent of a specific injury, had been established before the beginning of our period[1]. But it applied solely to torts, such as Trespass, Deceit, and Nuisance. The very word *damnum* implied a wrongful act.

Furthermore it is clear, although the Register does not supply any original writs of contract other than those of Debt, Covenant, Account and Annuity, (unless we include Contribution among contractual writs), that, by means of the notion of tort, a new branch of the law of contract was really establishing itself. The direction given to the Clerks of the Chancery in the famous 24th chapter of the Statute

---

[1] Fitzherbert, 98 M, and see precedents in Rastell's *Entries*.

of Westminster II. had resulted in a new form of action known as the Action on the Case, or Trespass on the Case. As the latter name implies, it followed pretty closely the viscontiel writ of trespass. It did not contain the special words *vi et armis*, the distinguishing mark of the royal writ[1], though it did conclude with the words *contra pacem nostram*[2].

A casual glance at the pleadings in Case in Rastell's *Entries* will shew the various uses to which the action had been put at the beginning of our period. An action on the case could be brought against an attorney who made default in an action which he was retained to defend, or a counsellor who divulged professional secrets; against a barber who shaved negligently; against a carrier who failed to deliver the goods entrusted to him; against a stable-keeper who so negligently kept a horse that it deteriorated in value; against a man who dug trenches across the road, so that the plaintiff could not get to his common; against a man who tore another's deed when it was not in his (the owner's) possession; against the vendor of an unsound horse who had (verbally) warranted it sound; against churchwardens who neglected to repair a gutter which they were bound by custom to keep in repair; against a sheriff who made a false return to a writ; against the utterer of slanderous words and the publisher of libellous matter; against a man who so negligently planted thorns on the plaintiff's land that

---

[1] Fitzherbert, 86 H.   [2] *ib.* 92 E.

they decayed and died; against a man who turned cats into another's warren[1].

In regard to many of these cases the tortious character of the act is obvious. The man who digs trenches across a road, the man who tears another's deed, and the man who speaks evil words and publishes malicious writings, are obviously guilty of moral trespass, which would be legal trespass but for the technical difficulty that it does not interfere with the plaintiff's corporeal possession. But why should the carrier who has failed to deliver goods, the sheriff who has made a false return, the attorney who has made default in a suit, the stable keeper who has neglected the horse, the vendor who has verbally warranted his property, the man who has negligently planted thorns—why should they be liable in this action? Their acts cannot by the strongest efforts be included under any reasonable definition of trespass. In some cases they do no act at all, merely omit to do something.

There are two answers to this question. In the first place, the defendant may be liable because he is held bound by law, in a society which is only emerging from the status-stage, properly to fulfil the calling which he professes to follow. The carrier, the sheriff, the attorney, the innkeeper, are recognized figures in the social drama; and if they do not perform their parts properly, they may be held responsible. They should not have professed their

---

[1] This seems, however, to be a pure action of trespass. The words *vi et armis* are in the writ.

callings unless they were capable of performing them. This class of persons, whom we may perhaps speak of as being bound by *quasi-contract*, was peculiarly the object of the Action on the Case[1]. For, as Fitzherbert observes on this point, "it is the duty of each artificer to perform his art duly and truly as he ought[2]."

But there are evidently some of the cases to which this explanation will not apply. Why hold the stable-keeper liable for neglecting the horse, or the man who planted the thorns badly? There was no previous duty on these defendants to do anything in connection with the subject matter. The answer is, to modern ideas, obvious. These persons are liable because they have *undertaken* the duties which they have failed to perform. "The said J. L. by his attorney R. F. complains that the aforesaid N. on the 12th day of September in the 21st year of the now king, *undertook* to keep well and sufficiently a certain horse belonging to the said J. (*ad quendam equum ipsius J. bene et competent' servand'* ASSUMPSIT) at C. aforesaid, and that the said N. so negligently and improvidently there kept on the day and year aforesaid the said horse, that the said horse greatly deteriorated, whence he says that he suffers loss &c.[3]" The defence is not a demurrer, but simply a denial of the negligence[4], and a request for a jury.

---

[1] "Persons that undertake a common trust." (Hale, *Analysis*, § 41).

[2] 94 D.   [3] Rastell, fo. 3.

[4] Down to Noy's time "not guilty" was a proper plea in Assumpsit (Noy, 56).

The pleadings are the same in the case of the thorns, and yet the gist of the action is, evidently, the *assumpsit*, or as it is sometimes more fully expressed, *super se assumpsit*.

The importance of the action of Case for our purpose is manifest when we notice that it was beginning, in Rastell's time, to be used as a substitute for the actions of Debt and Detinue. Rastell gives three examples of the former tendency, and two of the latter[1].

The three former are distinctly cases of assumpsit. In the first the defendant has undertaken, upon the plaintiff marrying one *A*, the defendant's servant, to give the plaintiff £10, and to pay the expenses of the wedding feast. The words are—*super se assumpsit, et eidem R fideliter promisit*. The marriage has been duly solemnized and the expenses incurred, but the defendant refuses to pay. In the second, executors of a deceased farmer seek to recover what at first looks like the balance of a simple money debt for goods sold. But it turns out at the last that they specially claim a sum of £20, as unliquidated damages for the loss which they have been put to in their administration by the defendant's failure to pay. In the third, a carpenter sues the administrator of a deceased person on an express assumpsit of the latter, to the extent of £3 15s. for work and labour done, goods sold, and money paid; but he also adds an unliquidated claim for money damages. In this case the words are only *super se*

[1] *Action sur le case in lieu de action de dett. Action sur le case en lieu de action de Detinewe.* (Rastell, *Entries*, ed. 1596, fo. 4.)

assumpsit, without adding *ac fideliter promisit*. But in all three cases there is a special allegation of fraud against the defendant, or the person whom he represents—*machinans fraudulenter decipere et defraudare, machinans et subdole intendens falso et fraudulenter totaliter decipere et defraudare, machinans callide falso deceptive et fraudulenter decipere et defraudare*[1].

The instances of Case in lieu of Detinue are equally instructive. In the first, the plaintiff counts that he lost certain articles of jewellery, and that the defendant found them, and that then the defendant, knowing that they were the plaintiff's (? if this was material) sold them, *et denarii inde provenient in usum et commodum proprium ipsius W.* (the defendant) *adtunc et ibidem convertit, ad damnum &c*[2]. The second case is not very clear, but it seems that a third person had bargained and sold to the plaintiff (who was one of the Justices of the Common Bench and proceeded by writ of privilege) some land of which the title deeds had been deposited with the defendant for safe custody, and at the sale the vendor had directed the defendant to hold the deeds "to the proper use" of the plaintiff, but the defendant refused to give them up. Apparently the case happened before the Statute of Uses[3], and so the plaintiff's interest in the land, as well as in the title deeds, would be equitable merely. Apparently, therefore, he could not bring detinue. But he brought his action on the Case for damages[4].

---

[1] Rastell, *Entries*, fo. 4.   [2] Rastell, *Entries*, fo. 4.
[3] 27 Hen. VIII. c. 10.   [4] Rastell, *Entries*, fo. 5.

Do not these five cases tell a plain tale ? In the first three, the plaintiff cannot bring Debt, because he asserts an unliquidated claim for damages; but he sues on a fraudulent breach of an undertaking. In the fourth, he cannot bring Detinue, because the goods are not in the defendant's hands; and, in the fifth, he is barred of that form of action because the title to the goods is not in him. But the law gives him a remedy on the Case. In other words, the original action of Debt first gave birth to the action of Detinue; then again it adopted Assumpsit, whilst Detinue adopted Trover. And so we get our new actions of Assumpsit and Trover, both really forms of Case, but rapidly superseding Debt and Detinue respectively. In the old *Natura Brevium* there is no writ of Case at all; in Fitzherbert, there is only one example of assumpsit[1] and one of trover[2]; by the time we reach Rastell (1564) the actions of assumpsit and trover have become sufficiently common to have evolved precedents of pleading, and in the year 1602, it was solemnly decided, by all the judges of England, in *Slade's Case*[3], that it was the plaintiff's option to choose assumpsit or debt, in cases where the latter properly lay. And it was resolved "that every contract executory imports in itself an *assumpsit*." As to the objection that by choosing the remedy of assumpsit the plaintiff would deprive the defendant of his wager of law, the Court agreed that this was no objection—"for now experience proves that men's consciences grow so large that the respect of their

[1] Fitzherbert, 93 F.   [2] *ib.* 94 A.   [3] 4 Rep. 92 b.

private advantage rather induces men (and chiefly those who have declining estates) to perjury." It had been previously held that an assumpsit lay upon an *express* promise to pay a debt due on a bond[1].

For some years the tortious origin of the new action continued to be admitted. In a case decided in 1665, Wyndham, J., allowed the plea of "not guilty" to a count in assumpsit, "for it is Trespass on the Case[2]." But, in the following year, the Courts held that a writ framed in assumpsit abated on the death of one of the two defendants "as in the case of Executor sued on a Contract....but otherwise in Cases of Trespass[3]." And so its contractual character seems to have been established; the great advantages which it possessed over Debt being its freedom from wager of law, and its applicability to those cases in which, from want of privity between the parties, the latter form of action could not be brought. It is noteworthy, however, that in these cases the plaintiff could not use the *indebitatus* count, but was obliged to state his case specially[4].

Now comes the important question. Could this

[1] *Ashbrooke v. Snape*, Cro. Eliz. 240 (1591). Professor Ames has some interesting remarks on the relationship between "past" considerations and the *indebitatus* count in Assumpsit (*Harvard Law Review*, 1888, p. 54 sq.).

[2] *Elrington v. Doshant*, 1 Levinz, 142.

[3] *Wirrall v. Brand*, 1 Levinz, 165.

[4] *Vide* Salkeld's note to *Hodges v. Stewart* (Salkeld, 125). And see the distinction taken by Littledale, J., in *Burnett v. Lynch* (5 B. and C. 609), between "Assumpsit" and "Action on the case founded in tort." The distinction had, however, been taken by Coke, at the beginning of the 17th century (*Pynchon's Case*, 9 Rep. 89 *a*).

claim on assumpsit be supported in all cases, or was it confined to a special class or classes of under-takings? There have been two suggestions which endeavour to restrict the limits of the action.

In the first place, some writers attempt to draw a distinction between malfeasance, misfeasance, and non-feasance; maintaining that the action was first introduced only for the former ground of claim, and was afterwards irregularly extended to the other two. This may very well have been the course of evolution at an earlier period, but it will not hold for that we are now considering. At the very beginning, the latest and least tortious of the three grounds, that of non-feasance, was clearly recognized as the basis of assumpsit. The sole example of the action given by Fitzherbert is of this character[1]. Rastell's precedents cover all three grounds indiffer-ently. It is clear, then, that we must postpone our examination of this part of the subject to a later chapter.

The other suggestion is, that the claim on as-sumpsit could only be supported when it was based on a consideration given for the undertaking. The suggestion, as we shall afterwards see, had been made before our period begins; but in a tentative way merely, and evidently the question was not fully settled when the Year Books ceased. We shall be justified, therefore, in examining a few of the best known authorities at different dates, to trace the growth of the doctrine.

At the very beginning of the period, there is an

[1] *Natura Brevium*, 94 A.

elaborate discussion upon the point in the Second *Dialogue of the Doctor and Student*, published in the year 1530[1]. The context of the discussion is well worthy of notice. An explanation of the learning of Uses has led the common lawyer to speak of *a nude or naked promise*, upon which, as he says, no action lies at law. Hereupon the canonist, waiving his former point, demands an explanation of the phrase, and the common lawyer proceeds to give it.

"A nude contract is," he says, "when a man maketh a bargain, or a sale of his goods or lands, without any recompense appointed for it...And a nude or naked promise is, where a man promiseth another to give him certain money such a day, or to build an house, or to do him such certain service, and nothing is assigned for the money, for the building, nor for the service; these be called naked promises, because there is nothing assigned why they should be made; and I think no action lieth in those cases, though they be not performed. Also if I promise to another to keep him such certain goods safely to such a time, and after I refuse to take them, there lieth no action against me for it. But if I take them, and afterwards they be lost or impaired through my negligent keeping, there an action lieth."

Accepting this statement for the moment, the canonist then starts a point of casuistry—whether the promisors in such cases are "bounden in conscience to perform their promise, though they cannot be compelled thereto by the law, or not." The

---

[1] Second Dialogue, caps. 23 and 24.

common lawyer naturally turns over the resolution
of this point to the divine, who proceeds to unravel
it in his own fashion. In the case of an ordinary
promise "so naked, that there is no manner of
consideration why it should be made, then I think
him not bound" (i.e. in conscience) "to perform it :
*for it is to suppose that there were some error in the
making of the promise.* But if such a promise be
made to an university, to a city, to the church,
to the clergy, or to poor men of such a place, and
to the honor of God, *or such other cause like*, as
for &c....then I think that he is bounden in conscience
to perform it, though there be no *consideration of
worldly profit* that the grantor hath had or intended
to have for it." But then he adds the casuistical
distinction, that the promisor must have *intended*
to be bound by his promise, otherwise it will not
bind his conscience, even though it were made "with
cause."

Hereupon the common lawyer points out the
superiority of the common law, which recognizes
that it is impossible for a human tribunal to judge
of "the intent inward of the heart," and, according
to learned authorities, rules thus—"If he to whom
a promise is made have a charge by reason of the
promise, which he hath also performed, then in that
case he shall have an action for that thing that was
promised, though he that made the promise have
no worldly profit by it......And likewise, if a man
say to another, marry my daughter and I will give
thee twenty pounds ; upon this promise an action
lieth if he marry his daughter. And in this case

he cannot discharge the promise though he thought
not to be bound thereby; for it is a good contract,
and he may have *quid pro quo*, that is to say, the
preferment of his daughter for his money." And
he goes on to say that the law of England takes
no notice of *cause*, and that a man would no more
be bound by promises to an university or a church,
than to a common person.

Then the divine raises another interesting point.
" But what hold they if a promise be made for a thing
past, as I promise thee xl. lib. for that thou hast
builded me such a house, lieth an action there ?"
The common lawyer answers in the negative. Then
the canonist suggests the case of an agreement to
compromise a tort by payment of a fixed sum for
damages, reminding his interlocutor that here the
promisor is already liable to the promise. But the
common lawyer points out that this is an accord,
rather than a contract; and that upon an accord no
action will lie[1]. And he adds, further, that in
England no action upon the canon law will lie in a
spiritual court to enforce a promise of a " temporal
thing"; "for a prohibition or a *præmunire facias*
should lie in that case."

Doctor. " That is marvel, sith there can no
action lie thereon in the King's court, as thou sayest
thyself."

Student. " That maketh no matter : for though

---

[1] " Accord without satisfaction is no bar." It was held that
even " accord and satisfaction " was no bar to *debt*. Such a plea
could only be used when the action sounded in damages. *Alden
v. Blague*, Cro. Jac. 99.

there lieth no action in the King's Court against executors upon a simple contract[1]; yet if they be sued in that case for the debt in the spiritual Court, a prohibition lieth. And in like wise if a man wage his law untruly in an action of debt upon a contract in the King's Court, yet shall he not be sued for the perjury in the spiritual court, and yet no remedy lieth for the perjury in the King's courts; for the prohibition lieth not only where a man is sued in the spiritual court of such things as the party may have his remedy in the King's court, but also where the spiritual court holdeth plea, in such case where they by the king's prerogative, and by the ancient custom of the realm, ought none to hold."

If these extremely interesting passages really represent the state of the law at the beginning of the sixteenth century, the doctrine of consideration was rather more advanced at that date than we have hitherto supposed. There are six points worthy of brief notice in the chapter from which our extracts have been made[2].

1. The apparent distinction made by the common lawyer between "contract" and "promise," and the use of the phrase "simple contract." The distinction is not much insisted upon; but it seems to confine the term "contract" to the case of sale, while " promise " would seem to include any undertaking,

---

[1] Semble, no action of *debt*. At any rate, it was soon afterwards held that *assumpsit* lay against executors on a simple contract. *Norwood v. Read*, Plowd. 179, and *Pynchon's Case*, 9 Rep. 186.

[2] i.e. cap. 24 of the Second Dialogue.

a practice which recalls the distinction between the 4th and the 17th sections of the subsequent Statute of Frauds. But it seems that the distinction was not religiously observed; for the nearly contemporary *Termes de la Ley* of John Rastell defines Contract thus[1]—" Contract is a bargayn or covenant between two parties, where one thinge is geeuen for another, which is called *quid pro quo*, for if a man make promise to me that I shal have xx.s. and that he will bee debtour to mee thereof, and after I aske the xx.s. and he will not deliuer it, yet I shall neuer haue no actyon for to recouever this xx.s. for that this promise was no contracte but a bare promise. *Et ex nudo pacto non oritur actio:* but if anye thinge were geūe for the xx.s. though it were not but to the value of a peny, *thē it was a good contracte.*" Evidently the tradition of the action of debt is still powerful. The use of the word " simple " as distinguished from " specialty " (though the latter term is common enough) is believed to be rare at this epoch. The *Termes de la Ley* is very loose in its definition of " Covenant," but it expressly confines the writ of Covenant to cases of " indentures ensealed," and it goes on to say—" And note well, that no writ of[2] covenaunt shal be mayntenable wythout especialty, but in the Cytie of London, or in other suche place privileged, by the custome and use[3]." There does not appear to be any definition of " specialty."

---

[1] Sub. tit. " Contract."

[2] The translation of 1575 says " or "; but this must be a misprint.

[3] *Termes de la Ley*, sub. tit. " Covenant." It is somewhat curious that Lord Mansfield, in *Pillans v. van Mierop*, did not refer to the custom of London.

2. The distinction between "consideration of worldly profit" and "cause" is well marked in the Dialogue. And it should be noticed by those who say that the economic doctrine of consideration came to us through the canon law, that the divine here expressly repudiates it, or, at any rate, treats it merely as evidence of genuineness. The canonist doctrine is evidently that of the Roman law. The circumstances of the bargain, not the bargain itself, are the important matters. But it may be noticed that a contemporary critic of the Dialogue points out that a parol grant of a rent for a sum of money will be helped in Chancery by a subpœna, "inasmuch as he that sold the rent hath *quid pro quo.*" But if the grant be voluntary, Chancery will not help him[1].

3. We notice also the clear recognition of the doctrine that the detriment to the promisee is just as genuine a consideration as the benefit to the promisor. The examples given are interesting. "If a man say to another, heal such a poor man of his disease, or make a highway, and I shall giue thee thus much, and if he do it, I thinke an action lieth at the common law."

4. There is the point of the past consideration put by the canonist, which was afterwards so clearly recognized in *Hunt v. Bate*[2], *Jeremy v. Goochman*[3], *Barker v. Halifax*[4], and *Docket v. Voyel*[5].

---

[1] *Treatise Concerning Writs of Subpœna*, Cap. III. [Printed from Cotton MSS. in 1815. Sweet.]

[2] Dyer, 272 *a* (1559). [3] Cro. Eliz. 442 (1595).

[4] *ib.* 741 (1600). [5] *ib.* 885, (1602).

5.   We have the express assertion of the common
lawyer that voluntary contracts are not enforceable
in the spiritual courts, although there is no remedy
on them in the king's courts.   This doctrine is
entirely consistent with the provisions of the Constitutions of Clarendon[1], though a little hard to
reconcile with the language of Glanville[2].   It is important to bear this point in mind in estimating the
influences at work upon the doctrine of consideration.

6.   We notice also the position of executors
with regard to the enforcement against them of
liabilities incurred by the testator.   They cannot be
sued in Debt on simple contract.   But it seems to be
admitted by an earlier part of the Dialogue that an
action of Debt on a specialty lies against the executors[3], presumably because the wager of law could
not be opposed to a specialty.   And, forty-six years
later than the generally assumed date of the *Doctor
and Student*, it was fully recognized that assumpsit
lay against the executors on a parol debt[4].   The
latter fact, no doubt, accounts largely for the increased
popularity of the action upon Assumpsit.

Merely dealing now with the general doctrine
of the necessity for a consideration to support a
simple contract, at any rate in assumpsit, we may
notice that Saint Germain's treatise is confirmed by
the arguments and judgment in 1565 of the Court

[1] *Constitutions of Clarendon*, cap. 15 (Stubbs, p. 140).
[2] Lib. x. § 12.   Perhaps Glanville only meant to say that the
Courts Christian could punish the defaulter *pro salute animae*.
[3] II. cap. xi.
[4] *Norwood v. Read*, Plowd. 179.   *Pynchon's Case*, 9 Rep. 186.

of Queen's Bench in the great case of *Sharington v. Strotton*[1] (which will be more fully dealt with on the subject of conveyance), by the forms of counts in assumpsit in Coke's *Entries*, published in 1614 (which always carefully specify the consideration), by Noy's *Maxims*, composed previously to 1641[2], by Hale's *Analysis of the Civil Law*[3], composed before 1676, and by Vidian's *Exact Pleader*, published in 1684[4]. After this, no authority is required for the general doctrine. We may close this part of the subject by referring to one or two important points decided upon it in the sixteenth and two following centuries. This will enable us to judge how far the preparation for the doctrines of the last chapter had proceeded.

1. The position of consideration as the test of the validity of the contract was very clearly brought out by the decision in *Nurse v. Barns*, a case of the year 1663[5]. In that case the plaintiff had hired certain mills of the defendant by parol contract for a term of six months at the price of £10. After he had moved in his stock, the defendant refused to allow him to remain in possession. The jury assessed the damages at £500, although it was

---

[1] Plowden, 309 *a*.

[2] No. 24, and cap. XLII. and the same author's *Dialogue on the Law*, p. 44.

[3] Sect. XLI., "Promises for a good consideration."

[4] At pp. 12, 14, 70, 51, &c. Even the counts for Breach of promise of marriage, for non-payment of a bill of exchange, and on policies of marine insurance, carefully specify the consideration. (Vidian was one of the Clerks of the Papers in the King's Bench.)

[5] Sir Thos. Raymond, 77.

admitted that the £10 was the fair rental value
of the mills. The court refused to disturb the
verdict. From that time it has never been doubted
that the amount of the consideration is no measure
of the damages for breach of the contract.

2. The question of the *genuineness* of the consideration was much discussed in the period. It was
very soon laid down that an existing enforceable
debt, or a balance on account stated, is always a
sufficient consideration to support a promise to pay
it[1]; and this doctrine soon led to the further rule
that the promise might be implied in such cases,
and so that *indebitatus assumpsit* would lie wherever
Debt could be brought[2]. This completed the doctrine
previously started in *Slade's Case*[3], and, practically,
gave its death-blow to the action of Debt.

With regard to considerations which consisted of
the withdrawal of claims or legal proceedings, the
courts were long undecided. On the one hand, it
was held that a promise to forbear (without naming
a time)[4], or to "relinquish" a suit (without alleging
that it was sound, or that it could not be raised
again)[5], or to abandon a claim manifestly untenable[6],

---

[1] *Hodge v. Vavisour*, III. Bulstrode, 222 (1617), and *Johnson v.
Cullamore*, *ib.* 208.

[2] *Butcher v. Andrews*, Salk. 23, *Walker v. Walker*, Holt, 328,
and see Salkeld's note to *Hodges v. Steward*, at p. 125.

[3] 4 Rep. 92 b (1602).

[4] *Philips v. Sackford*, Cro. Eliz. 455 (1596).

[5] *Ross v. Moss*, Cro. Eliz. 560. But see *Bidwell v. Latton*,
Hob. 216.

[6] *Tooley v. Windham*, Cro. Eliz. 206. *Smith v. Jones*, Yelv.
184.

were not genuine considerations to support assumpsit.
On the other, the allegation of a promise, followed by
forbearance, *per magnum tempus*[1], or to forbear *per
paululum tempus*, followed by actual forbearance[2],
were, ultimately, held sufficient. Upon the other
points of genuine consideration, the decisions are
somewhat hard to reconcile. For example, when
the defendant pleaded in bar of assumpsit that it
was agreed that in consideration that the plaintiff
should have two leases he would forbear his claim,
the plea was held bad on it appearing that the leases
were already vested in the plaintiff at the time of
the alleged agreement[3]. It was also decided that a
promise to pay a debt, due on the 1st November, on
the 3rd following, was no consideration for a promise
by the defendant to deliver up a bond and letter of
attorney[4]. On the other hand, it was held that a
payment of £4 when £5 were due was a proper
consideration for a promise to enter satisfaction of
a debt[5], that a promise to pay a debt on the day on
which it fell due was consideration for a promise
to deliver the bond on which it was secured[6], and
that a promise to pay the sheriff his lawful fees was
valid, although the only consideration for it was a
promise by the sheriff to do that which he was
already bound to do by law[7]. And a mother's promise

[1] *Mapes v. Sidney*, Cro. Jac. 683.

[2] *Cooks v. Douze*, Cro. Car. 241 (1632).

[3] *Oneley v. Earl of Kent*, Dyer, 355 *b* (1577).

[4] *Greenleaf v. Barker*, Cro. Eliz. 193 (1590).

[5] *Reynolds v. Pinhowe*, Cro. Eliz. 429 (1596).

[6] *Flight v. Crasden*, Cro. Car. 8 (1625).

[7] *Stanton v. Suliard*, Cro. Eliz. 654 (1599).

to persuade her husband to allow their daughter to
marry the defendant was held a sufficient consideration for a promise to pay money after the marriage[1].
But where *A* was indebted to the plaintiff and the
defendant to *A*, and *A* wrote to the defendant
requesting him to pay the plaintiff, it was held
that the plaintiff could not sue on the promise of
the defendant to pay if the plaintiff would promise
to forbear during a fortnight, because the plaintiff's
promise would not prevent him suing *A*, and he had
no right to sue the defendant[2].

3.   It was also laid down, long before *Lampleigh
v. Brathwait*[3], that a previous request validates a
promise given for a past consideration.   The doctrine
appears to have been first broached in an anonymous
case, reported under *Hunt v. Bate*[4], in 1568.   It
was agreed in *Hunt v. Bate* that a mere *voluntary*
courtesy would not support an assumpsit; but, in the
anonymous case, it was held that a promise " in consideration that the plaintiff at the special instance
of the defendant had taken to wife the cousin of the
defendant," was given for " good cause."   In a somewhat later case[5], plaintiff, at defendant's request, had
become surety for *X*.   *X* failed, and the plaintiff
had to pay.   Thereupon the defendant promised the
plaintiff that, if *X* did not repay him, he (the

---

[1] *Grisley v. Lother*, Hobart, 10 (1614).

[2] *Clipsam v. Morris*, 1 Levinz, 248 (1669).

[3] Hobart, 105 (1615).

[4] Dyer, 272 *a* (1568).

[5] *Sidnam v. Worthington*, Cro. Eliz. 42 (1585).

defendant) would.   And he was held liable.   This
decision was repeatedly followed[1].

4.   It was also clearly settled, that detriment to
the plaintiff is as good consideration as benefit to
the defendant.   In an undated case, reported in
Noy[2], in consideration that the plaintiff would forbear to sue X till his return to England, the
defendant assumed to pay what should be found
due from X.   The plaintiff forbore for three
months, and the promise was held binding.   This
is not a good case, as there was some reliance
placed on the fact that the defendant was X's
bailiff, or agent.   But in *Greenleaf v. Barker*[3], the
Court said—" Every consideration must be for the
benefit of the defendant, or some other at his request,
*or a thing done by the plaintiff, for which he labour-
eth, or hath prejudice.*"   And in *Bagge v. Slade*[4],
Dodderidge, J. observed—" If the consideration puts
the other to charge, though it be no ways at all
profitable to him, who made the promise, yet this
shall be a good consideration to raise a promise."
But when the plaintiff, at the request of the
defendant, delivered corn to the latter, who undertook to deliver it to X, but failed, the Exchequer
Chamber, reversing the Queen's Bench, held that
there was no consideration for the undertaking[5].

[1] e.g. *Beauchamp v. Neggin*, Cro. Eliz. 282; *Riggs v. Bulling-
ham, ib.* 715; *Townsend v. Hunt*, Cro. Car. 408; *Booden v. Thinne*,
Yelv. 41, all before 1615.

[2] *Martin v. Vaux*, Noy, p. 8.

[3] Cro. Eliz. 194 (1590).

[4] iii. Bulstrode, 162 (1614).

[5] *Riches v. Bridges*, Cro. Eliz. 883, and Yelv. 4 (1602).

This decision, which is quite inconsistent with *Coggs v. Bernard*[1], was, probably, always regarded as doubtful. The slightest trouble or inconvenience to the plaintiff, such as the submitting of an account to auditors[2], or producing the evidence of a debt[3], was held a sufficient detriment.

5. Another point of some importance was the clear recognition that the consideration for a promise might itself be a promise, and that in such a case it was not necessary for the plaintiff to aver, or even effect, performance. Thus, where the defendant, in consideration that the plaintiff assumed to deliver a bill of exchange, assumed to procure two sureties for the amount of it, it was held, on demurrer, that a plea that the plaintiff had failed to deliver the bill, was bad[4]. But, as Popham says[5], "Note here the promises must be at one Instant, for else they will both be nuda pacta." And, if performance of one promise clearly be made conditional upon the performance of the other, performance of the plaintiff's promise must be averred[6].

6. Certain considerations were already recognized as illegal, and the doctrine was laid down, that a consideration which is illegal in part avoids the contract, although there are unobjectionable

[1] Lord Raymond, 909 *n.*

[2] *March v. Culpepper*, Cro. Car. 70 (1628).

[3] *Loo v. Burdeux*, 1 Sid. 369 (1669).

[4] *Gower v. Capper*, Cro. Eliz. 543 (1597). And see *Martin v. Boure*, Cro. Jac. 6 *n.*

[5] *Nichols v. Raynbred*, Hobart, 88 (1615).

[6] *Oliver v. Evans*, 1 Levinz, 70 (1662).

items in it. Thus, a marriage brocage consideration
was pronounced illegal, and the House of Lords,
reversing the Lord Keeper, ordered a bond given
on such a consideration to be cancelled[1]. And it
was held, that money paid on an illegal consideration cannot be recovered as money paid to the
plaintiff's use[2]. So, where the defendant in consideration of two shillings paid, and that the plaintiff, a
bailiff, would release a prisoner (which he had no
right to do)[3], promised to pay the plaintiff the
prisoner's debt, the promise was held bad[4]. But
where part of the consideration was merely nugatory,
it did not avoid the contract if the rest were sufficient
of itself to support it[5]. The distinction between
considerations which are illegal and those which are
merely void, is elaborately discussed in a note to the
case of *Best v. Jolly*[6].

7. It appears to have been a moot point in the
period, whether a binding promise could be discharged without consideration, before breach. In
Treswaller v. Keyne[7] (1622) Haughton, J., said that
it might. And his ruling was followed in *Cook v.
Newcomb*[8] (1661), but there the whole contract was
executory, and the defendant had, consequently,
abandoned his rights. On the other hand, it was

---

[1] *Hall v. Potter*, Shower, 76.

[2] *Tomkins v. Bernet*, Salkeld, 22 (1693).

[3] Being forbidden by the 23 Hen. VI. c. 10, § 3.

[4] *Featherston v. Hutchinson*, Cro. Eliz. 199 (1590).

[5] *Coulston v. Carr*, Cro. Eliz. 847 (1601). *Bradburne v. Bradburne, ib.* 147. *Crisp v. Gamel*, Cro. Jac. 128.

[6] 1 Sid. 38.　　　　　　　　[7] Cro. Jac. 621.

[8] Sir T. Raymond, 42.

held that a liability on a tort could not be discharged by promise without consideration[1]. We have seen[2] that the doctrine of Haughton, J., is not now law.

Finally, we may notice, that the Courts fully recognized that a bill of exchange needed a consideration as well as any other parol contract, for they refused to allow a general *indebitatus* count upon it[3]. But it seems that, in an action on the special customs of merchants, a consideration would be presumed.

We now have to discuss the other branch of our subject, as affected by this period. And in studying the doctrine of Consideration in the law of conveyancing, we shall, in all probability, find that our best way will be to consider the question of conveyances of interests in land.

It will probably be admitted that the old common law conveyances of legal interests in land were quite innocent of the doctrine. "I would have one case shewed by men learned in the law," says Bacon, in his famous reading on the Statute of Uses, "where there is a deed; and yet there needs a consideration[4]." And so we may take it that the feoffment, the grant of incorporeal hereditaments, the Common Law Lease and Release, and the Confirmation, did not require consideration. *À fortiori*, the conveyance by

[1] *Covill v. Geffery*, 2. Rolle, 96 (1620).

[2] ante p. 36.

[3] *Hodges v. Stewart*, Salk. 125 (1691). *Meredith v. Chute*, Ld. Raymond, 759 (1703).

[4] Ed. Montague, xiii. 317. But it must be remembered that a feoffment did not, when Bacon wrote, require to be made by deed.

fictitious law suit—the Fine or Recovery—did not;
in fact, the recognition of a consideration would have
been inconsistent with the theory of such a conveyance. At the beginning of our period, the interest
of the lessee for years had only recently acquired a
place in conveyancing Law, by the invention of the
writ of *Quare ejecit*. No doubt, the notion of a lease
comprehended the notion of a rent, however small;
but there appear to be no traces of a lease ever
having been set aside for want of consideration. A
transfer of a leasehold interest was, probably, effected
by grant with attornment, and certainly such a
transaction could never be questioned for want of
consideration.

Nevertheless, the doctrine of consideration had
become of considerable importance in conveyancing
law at the time when our period opens. This
importance it had acquired by its connection with
the practice of Uses.

Many definitions of the nature of an Use have
been given, and much learned speculation has been
exercised to discover their origin[1]. One of the most
helpful and careful definitions is that suggested by
the counsel for the plaintiff (probably Plowden
himself) in the case of *Dalamere v. Barnard*[2],
decided in 1567. "The Use is not like a Rent
out of the land, but it is a Thing Collateral annexed
to the Person touching the Land, and is no more
than a Confidence for the Use of the Land, that is to

---

[1] Cf. especially the cases of *Lord Darcy* (Y. B. 27 Hen. VIII.
Pasch. pl. 22) and *Brent* (2 Leon. 15).

[2] Plowden, 352 *a*

say, a Confidence that the Feoffees, to whom the Land is given, shall permit the Feoffor and his Heirs, and such Persons as he shall appoint, to receive the Profits of the Land, and that the Feoffees shall make such Estates of the Land as he shall limit." In other words, a Use is a contract, but a contract of a very special kind. It is, in effect, a contract, express or implied, by the legal owner of an interest, that some other person shall have the practical benefits of such ownership.

Now it will readily be seen that such a contract as this is not only inconsistent with the principles of a feudal land system, but, if carried too far, absolutely fatal to the existence of that system. The feudal system proceeds upon the policy of imposing certain duties upon the notorious possessor of land. If the possession of land is a beneficial thing at all, it has so many compensating liabilities that the law will not recognize any dealing with it which is not open and ceremonious. The gist of feudal conveyances is, not consideration, but notoriety.

Accordingly, it seems to have been one view that the practice of putting lands to use dates from the passing of the Statute of *Quia Emptores*[1], which, in fact, gave the deathblow, in England, to the feudal system, though the health of that system had been previously undermined. Thus Pollard, in *Lord Darcy's Case*[2], says—"before the Statute of Quia Emptores, the tenure itself was a consideration."

[1] 18 Edw. I. st. I. c. 1.
[2] 27 Hen. VIII. 22. And see also *Abbot of Bury v. Bokenham,* Dyer, 8 *b.*

And it seems to have been held in *Cromwel's Case*[1] that an estate tail cannot be granted to *A* to the use of *B*, because the tenure itself was a consideration. But this is explaining an old difficulty by modern ideas.

Whether uses were actually introduced by the Statute of *Quia Emptores*, or not[2], it is quite clear that the practice of securing the legal and the beneficial interests in property had become common at a very early date. It is equally clear that the genius of the feudal law was averse to the practice, and very important to notice that this aversion was shewn by a series of steps culminating in the great Statute of Uses[3], intended to put the interest of the beneficiary, the *cestui que use*, as he was called, upon the same footing as that of a legal owner with corresponding interest. Whether or not the Statute of Marlborough[4], which aimed at preventing the loss of wardships by colourable feoffments, points to the practice, it is certain that the subsequent statute of Henry VII.[5], repeating the policy of the Statute of Marlborough, adopted the very term "use." The 50 Edward III. c. 6, which gives execution against the lands of those debtors who "donnont lour tenementz et chateux a lour amys par collusion davoir ent les profitz a lour volente," and then take sanctuary

---

[1] 2 Rep. 78 *a*.

[2] It is pretty certain that they were *not*. The writer has met with a case of land purchased *ad opus* as far back as the year 1225. (Maitland, *Bracton's Note Book*, Cases 641, 754, 1683, 1851.)

[3] 27 Hen. VIII. c. 10.   [4] 53 Hen. III. c. 6.

[5] 4 Hen. VII. c. 17.

to avoid personal execution, is aimed at the custom. And the provisions of the 50 Edw. III. are repeated by the 2 Ric. II. st. 2, c. 3, and the 3 Hen. VII. c. 4, in which latter statute it is clearly implied that there can be an use of goods as well as of lands. The 1 Ric. II. c. 9, seems to indicate that the practice of putting lands to uses was adopted by humble claimants to secure the assistance of powerful nobles; and the 7 Ric. II. c. 12, said[1] to be the earliest instance of the statutory adoption of the word "use," subjects the beneficial landed interests of aliens, as well as their legal estates, to the penalties of the Statutes of Provisors[2], while the 15 Ric. II. c. 5, brings lands held to religious uses within the operation of the Statutes of Mortmain[3]. Two statutes of the same reign exempted from forfeiture the lands held by a traitor "to the use and profit of any other[4]," and, on the other hand, subjected to forfeiture lands held to the use of a traitor[5]. The 1 Ric. III. c. 1, enables the *cestuis que usent* to convey their interests in such a manner as to bind the legal estate[6], and the 19 Hen. VII. c. 15, made uses liable for execution debts. Thus it will be seen that the Statute of Uses itself only completed a tendency previously existing.

---

[1] By Bacon, ed. Montagu, XIII. 327. Bacon's suggestion, (p. 329) as to the wording of the statute, is ingenious and probable.

[2] 25 Edw. III. st. 2, and 3 Ric. II. c. 3.

[3] 7 Edw. I. st. 2 &c. [4] 11 Ric. II. c. 4.

[5] 21 Ric. II. c. 3.

[6] It was held in *Dalamere v. Barnard* (Plowden, 352) that this power did not extend to donees of uses in remainder.

By these steps Uses had, at the commencement of our period, come to be looked upon very
much as *estates*. It is true that no notice of them
was taken by the courts of law, except in conformity
with express statute, but the protection given them
by the Court of Chancery caused them to be recognized in practice as almost equivalent to legal estates.
We are told by Littleton[1] that they were sufficient
to qualify for the position of jurors, and we gather
from the preamble of the Statute of Uses, that by
their means the power of devising lands was becoming general[2].

It was probably the refusal of the Courts of Law
to recognize uses as legally valid, that relieved them
from the trammels of formal phraseology. For the
Court of Chancery, at least at this period, prided
itself on its freedom from formality, and its power
of arriving at the meaning of the transaction. Even
the word "use" itself was not a term of art before
the Statute, whatever it may have been afterwards.
Any words, which expressed the intention of the
feoffor or legal owner to vest the beneficial interest,
were regarded as sufficient.

Nevertheless, it is clear, from the wording of the
early statutes, that at first uses were created by, or,
at least, with, feoffment. The equitable understanding accompanied the legal conveyance, and
arose from it. Thus appeared the class of uses
operating by transfer of possession. With these

[1] §§ 462—464.
[2] See the form given in Madox (No. cccliv) of a feoffment to
the uses of a will. It is of date 1506.

we have little to do; they were not very far removed from the common law doctrines of conveyancing.

But, at some date previously to the commencement of our period, the Court of Chancery had taken another, and very important step. It dispensed with the necessity of a legal conveyance as a foundation for the raising of a use, and held that, in certain cases, if the legal owner of an estate bound himself to convey, or attempted by ineffectual conveyance to convey that estate to another, he would be held to be a trustee of the estate for the intending transferee. Only in certain cases, however; for this arrangement was clearly a contract, and by this time it was beginning to be admitted that a contract required a consideration. Whether the necessity for a consideration was a rule originally evolved by Chancery or some other authority, we do not here enquire. We have seen that it was certainly known to, if not definitely accepted by the Courts of Common Law at the beginning of our period; and it is equally clear that it was then recognized by Chancery.

The consequence was, that if *A* agreed to sell, or, as the customary phrase ran, "bargained and sold," his freehold to *B* for a pecuniary consideration, the Court of Chancery held that *A* was seized of his freehold "to the use of" *B*, regarding it as against conscience that *B* should be deprived of all remedy, simply because he had omitted to take the formal feoffment[1].

---

[1] It appears that the separation of the "bargain and sale" from the formal feoffment was a recognized transaction in Henry VIII's time. (See Madox, Form cccLvi.)

It will be observed that, at any rate before the development of Assumpsit, this construction was really necessary to give *B* a substantial remedy, unless the bargain happened to be contained in a specialty covenant; for the action of Debt would, at the most, have enabled him to recover any money actually paid. But, by its subpœna, the Court of Chancery made the vendor a trustee for the purchaser[1].

This was the practice which, operating with such startling rapidity upon the words of the Statute of Uses, soon convinced the supporters of that statute, that, instead of closing the door against secret conveyances, they had actually guaranteed and encouraged them. For whereas the mere bargainee before the statute had only an equitable interest, after the statute he got a legal estate, and all necessity for conveyance was done away with. To obviate this startling consequence, was passed the Statute of Inrollments[2], but as that statute only applied to freeholds, it was soon evaded by the introduction of " Bargains and Sales for Years with Releases," conveyances framed on the old plan of the Common Law Lease and Release, but superior to it in not requiring actual entry by the purchaser[3]. In other words, secret conveyances of the legal estate at last became possible.

But, although the Bargain and Sale had thus

---

[1] Crompton, 43. (I have not been able to trace the references to the authorities.)

[2] 27 Hen. VIII. c. 16.

[3] *Lutwich v. Mitton.* Cro. Jac. 604.

become really a conveyance, its contractual origin was not forgotten. Though it was merely the formal initiatory step in the process, its framers were always careful to assign to it at least a nominal consideration, and the Courts held that the real consideration, which was usually expressed in the Release, might be extended to validate the Bargain and Sale, or, as it was frequently called, the "Lease[1]." And it was clearly admitted, in the great case of *Sharington v. Strotton*[2], that, as between strangers, no contract would avail to raise a use unless it had a consideration. But, if the use could not be raised, there could be no conveyance by effect of the statute.

Moreover, the doctrine of consideration, once admitted into conveyancing, soon made headway. By the middle of the sixteenth century it was said that a bare feoffment, without consideration, nothing being expressed about the uses, would raise an implied resulting use in favour of the feoffor, unless the feoffee were related to him by blood[3]. On the other hand, the process by which uses were being turned into estates was brought up against the counter-doctrine that a purchaser of the legal estate, without notice of the uses affecting it, was not bound by them, if he gave valuable consideration[4]. But, it

[1] *Barker v. Keat*, 2 Mod. 250. *Shortridge v. Lamplugh*, Ld. Raymond, 798, and Sanders (5th ed.) II. 79.

[2] Plowden, 298.

[3] Dyer, 146 *b*, in *Villers v. Beaumont*. Dyer dates the rule back to the Statute of *Quia Emptores*, but I prefer to take it as evidence of the law in his day. Madox shows no traces of the doctrine before Hen. VII.

[4] *Dalamere v. Barnard*, Plowden, 351 *a*. *Abbot of Bury v. Bokenham*, Dyer 8 *b*.

was said that the use itself could be assigned without consideration[1].

With regard to the minor point of the *statement* of the consideration, the law appears to have been pretty clearly settled during this period. It was decided that the Court must have positive evidence of the existence of a consideration, and so that the statement in a conveyance that it was "for other just and good considerations" was not sufficient[2]. On the other hand, it was held, after some doubt, that a conveyance might be supported by proof *dehors* of considerations not inconsistent with the terms of the deed[3], though it was not open to a party, or his legal representative, to deny the existence of considerations stated in the deed[4].

But one other very important point was also decided in this period. According to universal tradition, the assistance of the Court of Chancery in supporting uses created by mere contract was at first confined to cases in which the claimant had given valuable consideration. The Statute of Uses, however, is very sweeping in its language, and speaks of "bargain, sale, feoffment, fine, recovery, *covenant, contract, agreement,* will or otherwise," as the titles to uses. It is not surprising, therefore, that, in the unsettled state of the law on the subject of contracts and consideration, an attempt should have been made to support uses not based on

---

[1] Plowden, 351 *a.*

[2] *Mildmay's Case*, 1 Rep. 176 *a* (1582.)

[3] *Wilkes v. Lenson*, Dyer, 169 (Court of Wards, 1558.)

[4] Plowden, 298.

consideration. This attempt succeeded in the famous case of *Sharington v. Strotton*[1], to which it is now necessary to refer, and which is so admirably reported by Plowden, that there is every temptation to dwell on it.

Sharington v. Strotton was an action of trespass in the Queen's Bench[2]. The facts are as follows.

On the 3rd July 1559, *A. B.*, being seised in fee simple of the manor of Bremble, covenanted with his brother *E. B.*, for the avowed purpose of keeping the lands in the family blood and name, and for the "goodwill, fraternal love, and Favor which he bore, as well as to the same *E. B.* his Brother, as also to such others of his Brothers as in the same Indenture should be named," to stand seised of the manor to the following uses, viz.:

1. To the use of himself, *A. B.*, for life, *sans* waste.

2. To the use of the said *E. B.* and Agnes, his wife, and their assigns, for the term of their natural lives, *sans* waste during the life of *E. B.*

3. To the use of the heirs male of *A. B.* on the body of *F. L.* to be begotten.

4. To the use of the heirs male of (the body of) *E. B.*

5. To the use of *H. B.* (another brother) and the heirs of his body.

6. To the use of *H. B.* the younger (a half-brother) and the heirs of his body.

---

[1] Plowden, 298.

[2] The edition of 1816 says "King's Bench." But this must, surely, be a misprint.

A. B., the covenantor, died on the 21st February
1563, without having had issue by *F. L.*   Thereupon
E. B. and Agnes his wife entered.   The plaintiffs,
claiming under a fictitious lease alleged to have been
made by *A. B.* long prior to the settlement, also
entered upon the lands, and their possession was
disturbed by the defendants, acting under the orders
of *E. B.* and his wife.   Thereupon they brought
trespass, and, when the defendants pleaded the
settlement, demurred.

The argument for the plaintiffs was briefly this—
that the settlement was an attempt to create uses
without transmutation of possession, and therefore
required a consideration.   The plaintiffs' counsel
distinguished clearly between Motive and Consideration.   "The want of issue male is the Cause that
moved him to resolve, and the Resolution is but a
Demonstration of his Mind, and none of them is any
Consideration[1]."   Then they argued, that the only
considerations which could be alleged for the settlement were the desire that the lands should go to the
settlor's descendants, if any, and, failing them, to
owners of his name and blood, and, secondly, the
natural affection which he had for his brother.
Both which, they urged, were, as regarded the
settlor, mere motives, and not considerations.   For,
as they argued, with great force, the settlement
did not in the least confer upon the settlor any
power, or give him any advantage which he had not
before.   "Wherefore no new Thing is here done or

[1] Plowden, 302.

caused by the one Side, and there is no Cause here but what would have been if no such Covenant or Indenture had been made. But the Common Law requires that there should be a new Cause, whereof the Country may have Intelligence or Knowledge for the Trial of it, if need be[1]." They then argued, that the very object of the Statute of Uses was to ensure notoriety, as was evidenced by the speedy passing of the Statute of Inrollments; and it was hardly to be supposed that the framers of the latter Act, who would not allow a contract made with consideration to operate as a conveyance without enrolment, intended to authorize secret conveyances by contract without consideration.

On the other hand, it was argued for the defendants, that the Statute of Uses clearly recognized the acquisition of uses by contract, and, thereby, impliedly adopted the general doctrines of contract. And the defendants' counsel urged that, even supposing this covenant had been by parol, it would have been enforceable, the consideration being sufficient to support it. (To establish this argument they had to rely upon the speculations of Aristotle upon the Law of Nature, and other somewhat far-fetched authorities). But they contended, that this covenant, being by deed, required no consideration to support it, and on both grounds they claimed judgment. The plaintiffs' counsel do not seem to have been allowed a reply, or they might easily have disposed of the latter portion of the argument by pointing out that it might well be

[1] Plowden, 302.

that an action at law would lie for breach of the covenant, although it was not effectual to create an use[1].

The Court, however, adopted the first part of the defendant's argument, and held that the consideration of natural love and affection was sufficient, as between kindred, to support a covenant to stand seised. And this has since been recognized as the law, and is now accepted without question[2]. Indeed, so strict has been the deference paid to the precedent, that it has even been doubted whether a Covenant to stand seised can be supported by any other than a consideration of blood[3]. But these doubts have probably arisen from an anxiety to apply the Statute of Inrollments where there was a valuable consideration.

It is extremely probable, though difficult to prove, that the operation of the Statute of Uses, in executing conveyances made for money considerations without livery of seisin, was extended by analogy to the case of sales of chattels, and thus gave rise to the modern doctrine that delivery is not necessary in order to pass the property on the sale of a specific chattel.

---

[1] The defendants' counsel attempted to anticipate this objection by asserting that, as there was nothing executory in the covenant, the common law action would not lie (Plowden, 308).

[2] cf. e.g. Sheppard's *Touchstone*, 510 &c. Gilbert, *Uses*, 47, 48. Sanders, II. 97, 98. Fonblanque (5th ed.), II. 26. But the covenant to stand seised has, since the 8 and 9 Vic. c. 106, practically become obsolete.

[3] *Foster v. Foster*, Sir T. Raymond, 43 (1661). The decision is, however, inconsistent with what was said in *Bedell's Case* (7 Rep. 40 *b*) and *Henry Harpur's Case* (11 Rep. 24 *b*).

The results of this period may now be briefly summed up. At the commencement, the law is struggling with a difficulty of form. Certain classes of contracts are enforceable by particular actions, such as debt, covenant, account and annuity. But there is no general action on parol contract. Very soon, however, the courts begin to enforce verbal promises on the ground that, if the defendant has failed properly to perform a promise made to the plaintiff, whereby the latter has suffered loss, the defendant has been guilty of a tort, which will be punished by the award of damages. Hereupon, quite incidentally, another difficulty of contract-enforcement is got over, and the Courts can enforce, not merely a specific claim for money or chattels, but unliquidated claims, for which damages are the proper remedy. So popular does the new procedure become, that it soon almost swallows up the older forms of actions on contract, and establishes itself as the universal remedy for contractual claims. Its tortious character disappears entirely, or only remains in the beneficial feature of its applicability to un-liquidated claims.

But the conservatism of the courts has pruned the luxuriant abundance of the actions on assumpsit. From one source or another, one Court or another has derived the rule that a mere voluntary promise, unsupported by any return made to the promisor, or, in accordance with the new tortious action, by any detriment to the promisee, shall not be regarded as founding an assumpsit; and the doctrine has become generally recognized as law, in spite of some

doubts, when our period opens.   How and whence
this doctrine entered, whether from the older analogy
of Debt, or from some other source, whether by the
medium of Courts of Conscience, or by the rulings
of the Courts of Law, it is now our duty to enquire.

CHAPTER III.

THE EARLY HISTORY OF THE DOCTRINE.

WE are now about to consider a period of legal history which must awaken in the minds of all but a very few advanced students that respect which is due to the mysterious and the unknown. The available evidence for the period is scanty, and much even of that evidence is by no means reliable in detail. The earliest editors of the Year-Books were, doubtless, fully familiar with the forms and expressions of fourteenth and fifteenth century law. But the student who has to rely upon the seventeenth century edition of these invaluable reports, must necessarily indulge in a suspicion that his editors have often followed sight and sound rather than sense. It behoves him, therefore, to offer with the very greatest diffidence any suggestions which may be vitiated by his own ignorance and the incapacity of seventeenth century editors.

At the period which we have now reached in our retrospect, which may be fixed at about the year 1535, there seem to have been three ordinary remedies in the royal courts for the enforcement of contractual claims. These were the actions of

Covenant, Debt and Case. The actions of Account
and Annuity were special in their application, and
could only be used in certain well-defined circumstances.

The action of Covenant is generally assumed to
be immaterial to the doctrine we are considering in
this essay. It could, of course, only be brought
upon a promise under seal, and, except in the case
of the Covenant Real, which seems to have been an
early form of the action for specific performance, it
was simply a personal claim for damages. Its great
merits seem to have been that it did not admit of
the wager of law, that it could be brought against
the executors and administrators of the original
covenantor, and even against his heirs if these were
named in the covenant, and that no other proof than
simple production of the promise was required, at
least unless the defendant denied its authenticity.
On the other hand, the damages being an uncertain
quantity[1], the presence of a jury seems to have been
required from very early times, for the purpose of
assessing them. Moreover, the plaintiff was bound
to specify with particularity in his count each point
in which he alleged the covenant to have been
broken, instead of, as in Debt, merely claiming the
lump sum. In a case in the year 1405, Hankford, J.,
said—"In writ of Covenant he will recover damages
for each covenant broken...in which case he ought

[1] Professor Ames has pointed out (*Harvard Law Review*, 1888,
p. 56) that it is doubtful whether, before the 16th century, a
specialty promise to pay a definite sum or furnish specific goods
could be enforced by covenant.

to declare for certain in what points the covenants
are broken[1]." And the same rule was laid down in
an earlier case, of the year 1324[2]. But there seems
to be no trace in the Year Books of anything like
the doctrine of consideration in connection with
Covenant. And the author of Fleta, although his
reliability is, perhaps, questionable, expressly says
that "by a writing also anyone will be bound, so
that if he has written that he owes it, *whether money
was paid or not*, he is bound by the writing, and he
will not have an *exceptio pecuniæ non numeratæ*
against the writing, because he said that he owed
the money[3]." And elsewhere[4] the author of the
work explains that when he speaks of a writing
(*scriptura*), he intends a writing under the seal of
the promisor. Nay, if a man were careless enough
to lose his seal, and the finder fraudulently appended
it to a covenant, the innocent covenantee was entitled
to recover against the person whose seal appeared on
the covenant[5]. Evidently this doctrine is far away
from all notion of consideration.

In the much more common and useful action of
Debt, we shall find more to interest us. The action
of Debt is certainly as old as Glanville, whether or

[1] 6 Hen. IV. 8. (34). [References to the Year Books are always,
unless the contrary is stated, to the folio edition of 1678—9. The
first number after the name of the king is that of the page; if a
second follows in brackets, it is the number of the plea.]

[2] 18 Edw. II. 599.

[3] Fleta (Selden), II. 56, § 20.

[4] *ib.* II. 60, § 25.

[5] Glanville, x. c. 12. See also Britton, I. 29, 21. This rule
was actually followed in 8 John. (*Abb. Plac.* p. 56, Berkshire.)

no a special writ had in his time been invented for it, and it was in full use till the close of the 15th century. We must examine its nature with some care.

The writ of Debt was " general" in its character, i.e. it simply claimed of the defendant a specified sum which the plaintiff alleged that he owed to him. " Each writ of Debt is general" said Colepepper, J., in the year 1410[1], "and of one form, and the count special, and makes mention of the *contract, obligation, record*, etc." That is to say, the action can be brought on many grounds, or titles, but the form of the demand is the same in all cases. This exactly agrees with Fleta, dating from a century earlier, which says—"From obligations, promises and stipulations of this kind (i.e. writing, bailment, etc.) arises in the King's Court a certain action, which is called the plea of debt, which belongs to the King's prerogative, except they be debts arising from testament or matrimony[2]."

It would appear then, that Debt sometimes overlapped Covenant. In fact it was said in a very early case[3], that "one may have a writ of Debt in many cases where a writ of Covenant also lies." It is important, therefore, to ask what were the essentials in a good action of Debt. And this question is not easy to answer directly. The books seem to imply that two features must have been present in the cause of action. And there were, of course, essentials of proof.

---

[1] 11 Hen. IV. 73.   [2] Fleta, II. 60, § 27.
[3] 20 Edw. I. (Rolls Edition), 140.

To deal with the causes of action. It is fairly clear that Debt could only be brought for a specific claim, in fact, after the action of Detinue had been evolved as a distinct process, only for a specific money claim. A claim to unliquidated damages could not be made the ground of an action of Debt, though it might afterwards be added to a specific demand. In an action of Debt against executors for arrears of salary, the defendants objected that the writ had been purchased during the existence of another suit for the same claim. And the Court upheld the objection, Martin, J., saying—" In every case where by the writ the demand is certain, this is a good plea; as in *Præcipe quod reddat* brought for a carucate of land, to say that at another time the plaintiff brought another writ etc., and this writ was purchased pending the other etc., on which matter shewn he shall abate the writ; and the reason is simply that it is inconvenient that two writs shall be maintained for the same thing at the same time. *And so where one demands debt, the demand is certain;* but in writ of Trespass, it is no plea, and in such cases, where the demand is uncertain by the writ[1]." And in another case of the same year the plaintiff's counsel *arguendo* said " But debt is always for a certain sum," and the Court agreed with him[2].

But it would appear also, that Debt was properly confined to remedies for breach of contractual arrangements between the parties, though this rule

[1] 4 Hen. VI. 19 (5).
[2] 4 Hen. VI. 17 (3). The doctrine is certainly as old as 20 Edw. I. (Rolls, p. 140.)

may have been a mere procedural consequence from the older rule of a specific demand. In a case which occurred at the beginning of the sixteenth century, the mayor and burgesses of a town brought the action of Debt for the non-payment of a toll, alleging a prescription. The defendant pleaded that Debt did not lie, because the claim was "continuing." The plaintiff replied that the toll was "reduced to a certainty," and he instanced the case of a claim on an award of arbitrators given upon a demand for rent services and other matters, to which Debt did not, originally, apply. But the Court held the writ bad, one judge alleging as his reason, that "there was no contract between them[1]." It is clear, however, that this requirement of a contract was not stringently enforced, especially in statutory actions of Debt, e. g. that against a gaoler for allowing the escape of a prisoner. In fact, in very early times, the writ of debt savoured strongly of tort. ("That he tortiously detains from, or owes to him ten marks," etc.)[2]. And, though the writ would not originally lie for an unliquidated sum, it was beyond question that, in the 14th century at least, damages might be recovered in the action of Debt. Thus, in an action of Debt against a gaoler for permitting an escape, the plaintiff's counsel said—"We pray our damages; for in every case one shall recover damages upon a writ of Debt; and if one bring a writ of Debt on an obligation by Statute-Merchant the defendant

---

[1] 20 Hen. VII. 1 (2). And see also the expressions of Fitzjames, C. J., in 27 Hen. VIII. 24.

[2] 30 Edw. I. (Rolls), 234, 238.

shall render him damages." And the only doubt in the mind of the Court was, whether, this particular claim being founded on a statute which made no mention of damages, damages were given by implication. Ultimately, it was held that they were, and the plaintiff recovered his debt and 100 shillings damages[1]. The case is not, by any means, an isolated one[2].

Next we have to enquire how the scope of the action of Debt was limited by the rules on the subject of proof.

In some cases there could be no manner of doubt. If the plaintiff could produce a deed or a tally, *à fortiori* if he could refer to a record in support of his claim, the defendant could not plead the general issue, he had to shew that the proof was not in fact what it pretended to be. Thus, in the 45th year of Edward III., a man brought the action of Debt on a covenant by which the defendant promised to give him £100 if he would marry the defendant's daughter. The defendant raised the much-disputed question of jurisdiction, but he was overruled, on the ground that he could not go behind his deed[3]. The same law was held in 32 Edward I.[4], and in 20 Edward I.[5] it was said that a defendant could not wage his law against a tally, but that, if he denied it, the plaintiff must prove its reality.

In another case of the same year, where the

---

[1] 12 and 13 Edw. III. (Rolls), 354.
[2] cf. 42 Edward III. 11 (14) and 25 (10) and Britton, i. 29, 31.
[3] 45 Edw. III. 24 (30).   [4] 32 Edw. I. (Rolls), 184.
[5] 20 Edw. I. (Rolls), 68.

defendant produced a tally in answer to a claim on a recognizance, the plaintiff was compelled to wage his law, which looks as though the tally were considered as equal to the record in weight[1]. But the point must still be considered doubtful, for the reporter in the first case of Edward I. evidently disapproved of the ruling[2], and Fleta expressly says[3], that if the tally is not verified by suit, the simple oath of the defendant will be admitted in disproof, except in special places where other methods of verification prevail[4]. And then Fleta goes on to explain that it was this very weakness of tallies as a mode of proof which led to the creation of the security by Statute-Merchant[5].

An interesting and somewhat late case on the subject of proof in Debt occurred in the 39th year of Henry VI. The plaintiff brought his action in the Mayor's Court of London for £200, part of a larger sum of £500 due for the sale of cloth, he having agreed to receive the remainder in goods. The defendant offered to wage his law, but the plaintiff urged that, by the custom of London, he could not do so when the plaintiff shewed "bill or muniment written sealed and delivered by the

[1] 20 Edw. I. (Rolls), 330.

[2] *ib.* 68. And in the same year the proof of payment by the production of tally is said by the reporter to be a novelty (p. 304).

[3] Bk. II. cap. 63, § 12 (Selden). He is corroborated by 4 John, Pasch. (*Abb. Plac.* p. 387).

[4] e.g. the curious "oath on nine altars." It is pretty clear that Fleta was right about the necessity for suit. Cf. Maitland, *Bracton's Note Book*, Cases 177, 325, 645, 897.

[5] The Statute of Acton Burnel (11 Edw. I.).

defendant in testimony of the contract," and he produced specialty. The case was taken to the Exchequer Chamber, and Laicon, J., said—"It seems that the defendant (? plaintiff) shall be barred; for he should have brought his action on the specialty, and not on the contract." But Prisot, J., disagreed—"For the contract is not merged in the covenant, which is merely testimony of the contract[1]." The general opinion seems to have been, that the defendant was not deprived of his law, because the specialty offered differed in terms from the cause of action set up by the plaintiff. This case looks as though in the King's Courts the old force of documentary proof was giving way before the introduction of evidence in the modern sense, while it lingered on in the local courts. It does not seem to have occurred to the defendant's advisers to rely on the 38 Edw. III. Stat. I. c. 5, an enactment which looks as though the London courts had been pushing the rule of evidence beyond all legitimate bounds. But it must be admitted that the preamble to the statute is strongly in favour of the general view, that deed or tally was the only mode of proof in Debt then recognized which did not permit of an answer by wager of law.

We now come to the difficult question—Suppose that the plaintiff had neither record, deed, nor tally to shew for his claim, was he without remedy?

It seems to be quite clear that, at the end of the period covered by the Year Books, the action of debt could be maintained, although the plaintiff could

[1] 39 Hen. VI. 34 (46).

produce neither record, nor specialty, nor tally. Thus, it was the ordinary remedy to recover money due on a parol contract of sale[1]. It could be brought for board and lodging on a verbal agreement[2], on a bailment[3], or for arrears of wages due on a verbal hiring[4].

It is not, however, so easy to discover how the plaintiff proved his claim in such cases. The reports do not, as a rule, turn on questions of evidence, and though there was one point on the subject of proof which frequently came up for decision, this was a question raised with reference to the defendant's position, not, directly, that of the plaintiff. I allude, of course, to the point whether the defendant might "wage his law," that is, might bring a certain number of witnesses to swear that they believed that he did not owe the money. We have seen that this line of defence could not be adopted where the plaintiff shewed record, specialty, or tally. But it was sometimes refused also in cases where the claim was what we should call a parol one. Thus, an employer who compelled a man to serve him under the Statute of Labourers could not wage his law in an action brought by his servant to recover his wages[5]. And where a victualler brought an action for board against a prisoner in the Tower, the Court refused to allow the latter to wage his law[6]. But, as a rule, wager of law was the orthodox defence to an action of debt founded on a verbal contract.

This is an interesting fact, for it explains one or two difficulties. It is the key, for example, to the obscure question about the liability of the representatives of a deceased person. It is sometimes rashly asserted that Debt could never be brought against representatives, in their representative capacity, though it is admitted that, on bonds in which the heir was named, he could be made personally liable if he had assets by descent[1]. The fact seems to have been that the judges were at first inclined to allow Debt, subject to certain restrictions, against both executors and administrators. Thus, in the 22 Edward I., it was said that if Debt were brought against executors on tally or suit, the plaintiff must verify his tally, or tender his suit for examination, because the executors could not wage the deceased's law for him, "otherwise it would follow that the plaintiff would lose his debt," i. e., clearly, that if he could satisfactorily prove his claim, he was entitled to succeed[2]. And Debt was allowed against administrators in the 41 Edw. III.[3] Later on, however, the Courts seem to have drawn back, and, in allowing a claim in the 15th century, they clearly intimate that they only do so because the debt is verified by a certificate of auditors, who are made by statute judges of record, "and thus the action is brought

---

[1] 12 and 13 Edw. III. (Rolls), 168. The writ in this case is even in the *debet*.

[2] 22 Edw. I. (Rolls), 457.

[3] 41 Edw. III. 2 (6) and 11 Hen. IV. 73.

upon a record[1]." Seven years after this decision, occurs another which shews that the doctrine of 14th century has quite changed. A convent brought the action of Debt against executors, alleging that the testator had retained one of its members to sing masses for the soul of the deceased for a certain sum, and that the masses had been sung. The defendants pleaded that the testator, had he lived, might have waged his law; and the Court held the plea good, the plaintiffs being compelled to set up a confirmation of the bargain by the defendants themselves[2]. Fitzherbert, a century later still, denied that either Debt or Case would lie against executors upon a simple contract made by their testator, or that they could be made liable on a *Quominus* in the Exchequer[3]. Why? Obviously, because, as Knightly, who put the question, said, the testator could have waged his law in answer to a claim on a verbal contract.

Now comes the question—why was the defendant allowed to adopt this (to us) peculiar procedure in actions on verbal contracts, even when it was ridiculed by men like Coke? Surely it must have been because there was something corresponding with it in the plaintiff's mode of proof.

If we turn back to Coke, we shall find that he tells us, not merely that law can only be waged against a verbal contract, ("when it groweth by word,") but also that the oath is to be made with

---

[1] 4 Hen. VI. 17 (3).

[2] 11 Hen. VI. 48 (5).

[3] 27 Hen. VIII. 23 (21). It was said, however, that they could be made liable in Chancery, 7 Hen. VII. 10 (2).

eleven of the defendant's neighbours (*ipso duo-decimo*)[1]. Now, it is, of course, very tempting to suggest that the defendant required a clearance of twelve neighbours' oaths because the plaintiff proposed to convict him of the debt by a jury of twelve men *de vicineto*. But, unhappily for this suggestion, the wager of law seems to be a good deal older than the trial by jury or inquest; at least it was known before trial by jury became a common institution[2]. Again, though it is difficult to find warrant for the view in the Year Books, it seems fairly clear that the use of witnesses in the modern sense of the term was at least known at a very early date. Glanville contemplates the production of the attesting witnesses to a charter or instrument[3]. And the statute 13 Edw. II. cap. 2, provides a proper process for compelling such witnesses to appear. The 5 Eliz. c. 9, seems to have been the first statute dealing generally with the attendance of witnesses on a *subpœna;* but the statute treats the practice as well known, and, in criminal cases at least, the functions of the witnesses are alluded to in the well known rule laid down by the statute of Treasons passed at the accession of Edward VI.[4]

Whatever may have been the practice, however, towards the end of our period, it is clear that, in the fourteenth century, there existed a very special method of proof of claims which were unsupported by record or specialty. This was the *secta* or *suit*, to

---

[1] Co. Litt. (Thomas), III. 453.
[2] Cf. *Magna Carta*, ed. 1217, cap. 34, *nec ad juramentum.*
[3] Glanville, Bk. x. c. 12.   [4] 1 Edw. VI. c. 12, § 22.

which reference is frequently made in the Year
Books. In a very interesting case of the 15th year
of Edward II., two executors brought Debt against
an abbot, and demanded of him 40 marks 6 shillings
and 8 pence for divers causes, that is to say, 100
shillings by a writing, and 34 marks by reason of a
loan[1], *and for this they had good suit.* Devom (the
defendant's counsel) said—" What have you for the
debt?" Basset (plaintiff's counsel)—" In right of
the 100 shillings see this deed, in right of the
remainder, *suit.*" Devom, " Let the suit be examined on our part." Basset, " We have tendered
suit and are ready to prove it." Aldeburgh, J., "The
statute[2] wills that no man be put to his law without
testimony brought against him." It appeared, however, by the remarks of the Chief Justice (Bereford),
that the plaintiff had not suit after all, or at least
that it would not do its work; and the plaintiff was
fined for tendering suit on a false demand[3].

Before examining into the nature of the mode of
proof thus offered, we may remark that the references
to it only appear to cover a very short period. The
latest report which, so far as the writer is aware,
alludes to the practice, is of the 13th year of Edward
III.[4], and even there it is not clear that the proof by
suit is implied. Indeed, long before this, doubts had

---

[1] " per reson de aprest."

[2] i.e. Magna Carta (9 Hen. III.), c. 28.

[3] 18 Edw. II. 582.

[4] 13 Edw. III. (Rolls), 44. But it remained as a form of
pleading until the 16th century; and, which is very important,
it was used in the Action on the Case (cf. Rastell, *Entries*, pp. 9,
11, &c.)

been entertained of the validity of the process, for, in the 20th year of Edward I., an action of Debt was brought to recover the sum of £20, and in answer to the usual question—"What have you to prove the debt?" the plaintiff's counsel said—"Good suit," and the defendant appealed to the Court against the sufficiency of the answer. "We pray judgment if for such a sum we ought to answer on your bare suggestion (*a vostre vent*), inasmuch as you have neither writing nor tally to bring us to answer[1]." The Court overruled the objection, but the fact that it was raised seems to shew that the method of trial by suit was going out of fashion. It is true that the method was recognized in other cases of the same year[2], that it is described by Fleta[3], and that, on the other hand, Glanville, writing at the close of the 12th century, alludes to the *secta* as a protection against a prosecution for theft[4]. But the whole tenor of Glanville's tenth Book excludes the recognition of such a process as a proof of debt, and in fact, Glanville speaks of a bailment being proved *generali probandi modo in Curia, scilicet per Scriptum vel per Duellum*[5].

If we now ask ourselves, what was the *nature* of this proof by *suit*, which appears to have had such a brief existence, we find some difficulty in getting a satisfactory answer. One or two things may, however, be noticed.

In the first place, it is quite clear that the suit

---

[1] 20 Edw. I. (Rolls), 222.   [2] *ib.* 68, 304.
[3] Bk. II. c. 63, § 10.   [4] Bk. x. c. 17.
[5] *ib.*

was a different thing from the inquest or jury. We have the functions of the latter institution clearly indicated in a case of the 12th year of Edward II. Miles Hunt of Stratford brought a writ of Debt against Symond de J., and demanded of him 30 quarters of barley of the price of £20, shewing a deed in testimony of the debt. The defendant pleaded infancy, "but the inquest said that he was of full age" (at the time when the deed was made), and they were then asked what was the value of the barley at the time when it should have been paid. The inquest said, "At the time when he made the writing, the quarter was worth only three shillings; but when he should have paid it was worth twelve shillings." The Court—"Speak of the damages of the detinue." The inquest—"Damages, £10." (But this award was reduced by the Court on the ground that it was contrary to the evidence[1]).

If we turn now to Fleta's description of the suit, we shall see how different are the positions of the two institutions. Fleta is not, perhaps, a very good authority, but he is hardly likely to be mistaken in his description of a contemporary process of such importance. He tells us that the creditor who has no writing of the debtor's to shew for his claim, will not be able to make the latter answer *ad simplicem vocem*. But he may produce *secta*, "that is, the testimony of lawful men who were present at the making of the contract between them, and if they, on being examined by the judge, are found to agree, the defendant will then be able to wage his law

[1] 12 Edw. II. 375.

against the plaintiff and his suit." And this wager of law is explained to be a counter-oath of twice the number of witnesses (*testes*) offered on behalf of the plaintiff, the burden of proof being now shifted to the defendant. It is, perhaps, worth noting, that, in Fleta, the defendant's witnesses are spoken of as *juratores*, and that the maximum number which he can be called upon to produce is *twelve*[1].

It will have been observed that Fleta says that the suit may be examined by the judge. And, he adds at a later stage, "if the suit is found to disagree (*variabilis*), the defendant will not be compelled to wage his law, but the action will be dismissed, and the plaintiff will be liable to a fine." Upon the point of examining the suit, however, there seems to have been a difference of opinion, for, in a case of the 7th year of Edward II., the defendant asked that the plaintiff's suit might be examined, but the plaintiff objected that the Court did not allow this course, and his objection was admitted[2].

What was the *suit* which was thus produced ?

If we took Fleta alone, we might readily suppose that it merely consisted of the ordinary witnesses, in the modern sense of the term, to an oral transaction.

But the attitude of Glanville, a far more reliable writer, forbids this view; for Glanville, while he alludes to the *secta* as a thing well known, tells us, almost in the same chapter, that the King's Court is not in the habit of enforcing *privatæ conventiones*, at any rate as regards movables, unless they are made in the Court itself, i. e., are matters of record. And

---

[1] Fleta, II. 63, §§ 10, 11. [2] 7 Edw. II. 242.

if the creditor has neither *vadium, neque plegios, neque aliam diracionationem nisi solam fidem, nulla est hæc probatio in curia Domini Regis*[1]. No doubt, Glanville confined his observations to the new royal procedure, and it may well be that proof by suit was in existence in his day in the local courts. Britton, writing at the end of the thirteenth century, and describing the process to recover debts of less value than forty shillings (where the local courts were still allowed jurisdiction) says that the plaintiff may tender suit[2]. But it seems likely that the process came into the King's courts between the times of Glanville and Fleta, and it behoves us to consider if in any way we can account for its appearance.

The obvious suggestion is that it is due to the clause of the Great Charter (No. 28 in the statutory edition) which requires that *nullus ballivus de cetero ponat aliquem ad legem manifestam nec ad juramentum simplici loquela sua sine testibus fidelibus ad hoc inductis*. But it is to be noticed, that the words *manifestam nec ad juramentum* do not appear either in the "articles" on which the Great Charter was founded, nor in the first or second edition of the Charter itself. They are an emendation of the year 1217[3]. This fact is important.

It will be observed that the new provision, whatever it may be, was intended to operate primarily on

---

[1] Glanville, x. 12.   [2] Britton, I. 29, 12.

[3] Blackstone, *The Great Charter*, pp. 5, 17, 34, 43. Oddly enough, the emendations ultimately brought back the clause to the numerical position in which it was originally placed by the Articles.

ballivi. The term employed, taken in conjunction with the general character of the Charter, as an instrument designed to place limits on the royal power, will probably lead us to the conclusion that by the word *ballivus* a royal official is intended. The royal officials are no longer to place a man upon his law without the testimony of lawful witnesses. Obviously then they had been guilty of such a practice. On what pretext?

It can scarcely have been any other than the Assize of Clarendon, issued in the year 1166, barely fifty years before the Great Charter. This Assize is generally supposed to have introduced, as a regular practice, the sworn accusation of alleged offenders by a representative jury of the county before the king's justices. The procedure was inquisitorial, not litigious; royal, not popular. The presumption was, that a person accused by the solemn oath of such a body was guilty. Accordingly, the accused had to submit to the ordeal by water *and* to swear that he had not been guilty of the crime charged[1]. If he were already of bad fame, even this method of clearing himself was not allowed, at least unless he had a warranty[2].

Putting aside the tempting opportunity to speculate about the connection between this "warranty" and the later "wager of law," we may notice that the Assize of Clarendon tended to familiarize men's minds with the practice of accusation by sworn testimony, not indeed of witnesses in the modern sense, but of persons who professed to state their knowledge of the

[1] Ass. of Clarendon, 1, 2.   [2] *ib.* 12—14.

fact. It is also worth remarking that the very expressions of the Assize serve to connect it with the Charter. The Assize says that, if a man is already of bad fame, *non habeat* **legem**. The Charter says that a bailiff is not to put a man *ad legem,* without sworn testimony. The *lex* of the Assize consisted of ordeal and clearing oath.

From what we know of John, and the tendencies of royal officials in those days, it is not, surely, a strong suggestion, that the king's bailiffs had been compelling people to submit to the ordeal and oath on irregular accusations. A conviction under the Assize meant a profit to the royal exchequer. The royal exchequer was at a low ebb. What more natural than that the king's servants should endeavour to replenish it by irregular manipulations of the Assize, as we know that they did by irregular manipulation of treason-law, wardship-law, and the like ? If this were so, the 28th article of the Barons' complaint is intelligible.

But why the addition of the words *manifestam nec ad juramentum* in the year 1217 ?

Surely because there was a necessity for special precaution. The Charter was signed in June 1215. In November of the same year the fourth Lateran Council met in Rome, and formally abolished the ordeal as a mode of judicial proof. In the excitement of the closing months of John's reign, the fact that this abolition had made a substantial alteration in English criminal procedure would hardly be noticed[1],

---

[1] The latest instance of trial by ordeal which the writer has seen is in Trinity term of the 15th year of John (1213), reported in *Abbreviatio Placitorum*, p. 90.

or, if noticed, may have been disregarded by the baronial party, in their hatred of the Papal policy, which was now endeavouring to release the royal traitor from his Charter oath. But when affairs calmed down, and, after the hurried re-issue of the Charter at the close of 1216, the young king's ministers prepared for a more formal edition in the next year, they probably recognized the force of the conciliar declaration on the question of ordeals, and altered the wording of the clause. What the precise meaning of the epithet *manifestam* may have been, it is difficult to say[1]. But it is reasonable to suppose that the *juramentum* is intended to cover the *et juret* of the second clause of the Assize of Clarendon. The word *manifestam* may have been inserted for greater safety, in case the decree of the Lateran Council should be held inoperative. At any rate, we know that, either in spite of, or as the result of the Charter, the presenting jury became a permanent and essential factor in criminal prosecutions for graver offences.

One thing more must be said about the presenting jurors of the Assize of Clarendon. They were really *sectatores* or *suitors*, i. e. persons who were bound to follow the court[2]. Having been chosen for the purpose, they could not absent themselves. The word *suit*, is, then, peculiarly applicable to them.

But such a striking method of procedure as this could hardly fail of its influence on other depart-

[1] Blackstone (III. 344) treats the *lex manifesta* as trial by battle. *Sed quære.*   [2] Ass. Clar. 8.

ments, more especially if, as there is shrewd reason
to suppose, Henry II., like the able statesman that
he was, formed his presenting jury on a model
already familiar to his subjects. If there was
anything like the presenting jury in English procedure, we may be pretty sure that the Court of
Common Pleas, in its civil jurisdiction, would
soon make use of an institution familiar to the
local courts as well as to the Court of King's
Bench.

It seems reasonable to say that the Sale or
Transaction witnesses, mentioned in Edgar's *Ordinance*[1], and apparently alluded to by William
Conqueror in his legislation[2], are a good deal like
the presenting jury of the Assize of Clarendon. By
Edgar's *Ordinance* there were to be thirty-three
witnesses for every *burh*, and for every small burh
and hundred, twelve witnesses; and no sale of chattels
was to be conducted without the presence of two or
three of these officials. William repeats the prohibition, at least so far as relates to the sale of cattle
and *res vetustœ*.

No doubt the primary object of these provisions
was to secure evidence in accusations of theft. A
man who bought a chattel to which the vendor could
not make a title, ran a serious risk of being con-
demned as a felon. From such a fate the production
of the transaction witnesses would save him, and it is
probable that this was the point to which Glanville
referred in his mention of the *secta*[3]. But it will be

[1] Stubbs, *Select Charters*, p. 72.   [2] *ib.* p. 84.
[3] Glanville, x. 17, *id eum a felonia liberabit.*

noticed that these instances were specially connected with the hundred, as were the presenting jurors of the Assize, they even were of the same number (twelve), and it is quite likely that they were bound to attend the meetings of the hundred, just as the presenting jurors were compelled to attend the king's justices in the shire. And how very natural that such persons, in days and courts when and where criminal and civil business had not yet been specialized, should be used for the purpose of proving claims in debt, at any rate in cases which arose out of sale or bailment—in other words, that they should be the *secta* alluded to by Britton ? And if at first in the local courts, why not afterwards in the Common Pleas, encouraged thereto by the practice of the King's Bench in criminal cases ? A suggestion such as this, conjectural though it be, at least offers some solution of the difficulty that, when Glanville wrote, debts resting on oral testimony could not be enforced in the King's courts, whereas, when Edward was king, they could be proved by *good suit*.

Happily, there are records which make this a strong probability.

The interval between the time of Glanville and the beginning of the Year Books is mainly covered by the long reign of Henry III., the legal results of which are incorporated into the great work of Bracton. It is obvious, however, that Bracton had small respect for the suit, which he tells us was composed in his day of *domestici et familiares*, and did not make a proof, but only raised a slight presumption, which could be rebutted by proof to the contrary and by *defensio per legem*[1]. And he expressly excludes the suit from his category of *proofs*, which he divides into two classes of *vox mortua* or *instrumentum*, and *vox viva* or *patria* and *inquisitio*[2].

But although Bracton, writing with the advanced legal ideas of the latter half of the century working in his mind, is apt to make light of the suit, it is quite clear that it played an important part in the legal business of the generation which succeeded the granting of the Charter. The evidence (probably used by Bracton himself) exists in abundance in the great collection of early thirteenth century cases edited by Professor Maitland[3]. In these cases suit is used to prove all manner of facts, often, as we should think, to prove legal conclusions. Suit is used to prove grant of dower[4], proceedings in ecclesiastical courts[5], identity of parties[6], seisin[7], ownership of chattels[8], title generally[9], entry[10], commission of waste[11], absence beyond seas[12], marriage[13], death[14], taking of monks' vows[15], and a host of other things.

[1] Lib. v. cap. 1, § 9. Cf. also clear distinction between *probatio* and *presumptio* in iv. 9, § 2.

[2] *ib.* v. 1, § 8.

[3] *Bracton's Note Book*, edited by Maitland, 1887 (Pitt Press).

[4] *Note Book*, Cases 279, 377, 457, 518, 898, 941, 1065, 1102, 1390, 1848, 1919.

[5] Cases 646, 649, 665, 768, 910.   [6] Cases 247, 374.

[7] Cases 233, 1002. (It appears that seisin was sometimes given in the hundred-court, Case 754.)

[8] Cases 588, 1115.   [9] Case 385.

[10] Cases 451, 499, 1936.   [11] Case 739.

[12] Case 123.   [13] Cases 953, 1604.

[14] Cases 356, 546, 1307, 1311, 1595.

[15] Case 1586.

Moreover, in several cases the party is defeated, because he has nothing to prove his assertion, *nisi simplicem vocem suam*[1].

And it is evident also that modern notions as to the credibility of evidence are beginning to shew themselves under cover of the process. In one case the party offers to prove a gift of land by suit, to wit, *per Henricum le Sauvage et alios qui interfuerunt ubi ipsa* (the defendant) *donum illud ei* (the plaintiff) *fecit*[2]. And, in another, the plaintiff was defeated because the suit produced to prove a lease *non interfuit traditioni nec aliquid testificantur nisi de auditu*[3]; while, in spite of later doubts, it is clear that the suit could be examined, and that, if they materially disagreed, the value of their testimony disappeared[4]. But where suit is opposed by suit[5], or by deed[6], the Court obviously feels itself in a difficulty, which looks as though the practice of balancing conflicting testimony were still in its infancy. Perhaps this difficulty resulted in an increased use of the *recognitio*[7]; at any rate, it appears that about the year 1220 the alternative modes of trial were suit, battle and inquest[8], and it seems too that if the plaintiff produced suit, the defendant could not claim the inquest, unless he had

---

[1] *Note Book*, Cases 260, 425, 451, 494, 507, 528, 555, 575, 600, 660, 816, 1065, 1129, 1565, 1672, 1863, 1868, 1936.

[2] Case 116.

[3] Case 663. See also Cases 761, 890, 946.

[4] Cases 424, 649, 762, 1693, and see Bracton, Bk. v. 13, § 2.

[5] Case 1115. [6] Case 890.

[7] Case 890. [8] Cases 115, 116, 167.

something to rebut the presumption raised by the suit[1].

Finally, we must notice, in connection with the action of Debt, the very important doctrine of *quid pro quo*.

It is unfortunate that most of the later cases of the period which deal with this doctrine should also be involved in a separate and equally difficult question; but perhaps the connection is not accidental. In the 20th year of Edward IV. the action of Debt was brought to recover a sum of £20, which the defendant had promised to pay "on" or "with" (*ove*) the marriage of his daughter. A plea to the jurisdiction was taken and allowed by the majority of the Court (Choke dissenting). But Collow, one of the majority, said, " To my mind there is something else to look to, for in this action it must be shewn[2] that something shall be done to the advantage of the defendant, and, sir, it seems to me that, that notwithstanding, the plaintiff will recover, for this it will be in many like cases, as if I *make a covenant* with a man to build me a house, and that he shall have for his labour twenty shillings on a certain day, by which if he does not build the house, still he has the twenty shillings, and I have nothing for this; also, notwithstanding that the thing which the plaintiff shall do is to a third person, who is not privy to the contract, still it seems to me that it is good enough, for if I promise to R. N. £20 if he go to my Lord Brian, and

---

[1] Bracton, IV. 9, 2. But see *Note Book*, Case 1603, where, however, the plaintiff had only one witness.

[2] " uncore monstre "?

carry such a thing which is to the advantage of my said lord, I understand that I shall pay the £20, if he do the thing etc.[1]"

This is not very clear, especially with regard to the case of the house, which may turn upon the difference between Covenant and Debt. But the main argument appears to be, that if any advantage accrued to the defendant, the Court will hold him liable without asking why it is an advantage to him. It is enough that his request is gratified.

The point is much clearer in a similar case decided six years earlier, where the Court drew the rather fine distinction between a promise (like that in 20 Edw. IV.) to give £20 "with" the defendant's daughter (which was matter for the spiritual court) and a promise to give £20 "to the plaintiff for marrying his daughter," which, as the Court remarked, was a matter for common law, "because that he did another thing for this £20, so that he (the plaintiff) had *quid pro quo*[2]." By "another thing" is probably meant "something that he would not have done but for the promise." There are traces of this rather technical distinction at a still earlier period[3]. Between the decisions in the last two cases, the Master of the Rolls put the question to the judges of the Common Bench, whether, if a man promises to another a sum of money to marry his daughter or servant, and he marry her accordingly, he will have an action of Debt. The Court was much divided in opinion—

[1] 20 Edw. IV. 3 (17).
[2] 14 Edw. IV. 6 (3).   [3] 22 Ass. 101 (70).

Choke and Littleton thought not, but purely on the ground of the spiritual jurisdiction. Townsend came to the same conclusion, not only for that reason, but also on the ground that the promise was "nude," "as if I promise you twenty shillings to make your hall anew, here no action lies for this, for he has not *quid pro quo*: and it is not like the case where I promise you six shillings a week for the board of such a one, for there he has *quid pro quo, and the law understands that he is a person by whose services I have advantage.*" But Rogers and Suliard differed, saying that it was no nude promise—" for he had *quid pro quo*, being that his daughter or friend is advanced by the projected marriage[1]." The earlier cases are, on the whole, against the soundness of the action[2], partly on the ground of spirituality, but largely also on the absence of *quid pro quo*. It is evident, however, that there was much difference of opinion. In one case Moile, J., said, " and as to the objection that the action sounds in covenant, that is not to the purpose when the thing is done, as if I retain a carpenter to build a house, and that he shall have of me forty shillings for building it, now if the carpenter build the house aforesaid, he shall have a good action of Debt against me; and still this sounds in Covenant: for if he will not build the house, I shall (not) have an action against him without specialty, because it sounds in covenant: but when he has done the thing, then is the action to demand the duty accrued to him,

---

[1] 17 Edw. IV. 4 (4).

[2] 37 Hen. VI. 8 (18). 15 Edw. IV. 32 (14), and 45 Edw. III. 24 (30). But cf. reporter's note to last case.

for when the thing is done, that is sufficient for him to maintain the action[1]." The question of jurisdiction in these cases seems to have turned upon the construction of the *Articuli Cleri*[2], but the reason for the frequency of the cases at this particular epoch is not so easy to discover. Apparently, Bracton, who wrote long before the *Articuli Cleri* were published, is clear against the jurisdiction of the King's Courts[3].

But, whatever the cause of the appearance of these cases, we gain from them at least one valuable hint, viz., that in the latter half of the fifteenth century the Courts were strongly inclined to enforce a promise where the promisor had received a benefit therefor, and that they were unwilling to enter into an estimate of the precise nature of the benefit. And of the general necessity of *quid pro quo* for Debt at a still later period, there can be no manner of doubt[4].

The existence of the doctrine, however, does not of itself reveal the circumstances of its origin. The discovery of the circumstances is of course the very point of difficulty; and the writer does not pretend to offer more than a mere suggestion.

The suggestion is, that the doctrine of *quid pro quo* was in some way connected in its origin with the subject of evidence. The value of such a doctrine in this connection is well seen in a report of a case decided in 16 Edward IV., and previously referred to. The plaintiff brought Debt, counting that he had sold the defendant cloth, and that the latter had

[1] 37 Hen. VI. 8 (18).   [2] 9 Edw. II. st. I. cap. 1.
[3] Bracton, IV. 12.   [4] 27 Hen. VIII. 24 (3).

retained him to fit and cut divers gowns and hoods.
The claim therefore was, as we should say, partly for
goods sold and partly for work and labour.   The
defendant offered to wage his law for the goods sold;
and, as to the rest, he demanded judgment, on the
ground that the plaintiff should have alleged a
covenant.   But the Court said—"This is a natural
contract, for it well appears that the defendant had
quid pro quo[1]."   In other words, the admission by
the demurrer of *quid pro quo* supplied the place of
specialty evidence.

But there is another interesting point.   The
defendant's counsel admitted that if the plaintiff had
been a common labourer, included in the Statute of
Labourers, he would have been able to bring Debt,
and his admission is confirmed by earlier cases[2].   It
seems to have been regarded as only right that a
person who was compelled by statute to serve, should
have an effectual remedy for his wages, without being
made to produce a proof which, by the nature of the
case, he could not have insisted on obtaining.   In
other words, Debt is granted as a special privilege on
a parol contract.

A very early instance of the doctrine seems to
point to the same connection.   In the 12th year of
Edward III., an attorney brought the action of Debt
for arrears of salary, alleging a covenant engaging
him for ten years, at twenty shillings a year.   The
defendant's counsel objected—"This count begins in
covenant and ends in duty; judgment of such a

[1] 16 Edw. IV. 10 (3).
[2] 19 Hen. VI. 54 (15).   38 Hen. VI. 13 (30).

count is not warranted." He was overruled. Then
the objection was raised—" He has nothing shewing
the covenant." But Scarshulle, J., said—" If a man
counted simply of the grant of a debt, he would not
be received without specialty; but here you have his
service for his allowance, which lies in cognizance (*qe
chiet in conisaunz*), and you have *quid pro quo*[1]."
Whatever " conisaunz " may mean, whether it is a
technical allusion to the *recognitio*, or simply stands
for "knowledge," it is quite clear that it is the question
of proof which is being discussed, and that the Court
thinks the proof sufficient, because there is *quid pro
quo.*

Now, it may be asked, (to turn back and pick up
a former thread of argument),—Why did not the
plaintiffs in these cases rely on the *suit?*

The natural answer is, that the suit was not
available for transactions such as these, which did
not arise out of sales or bailments. The *suit* could
not swear to the matter, because it had not been
present. And if this suggestion be sound, it would
seem to shew that the doctrine of *quid pro quo* was
originally an expansion of a rule of evidence. At
first (in Glanville's time) only deeds and records
were sufficient. Then the *suit* was admitted, and
so parol contracts of certain kinds, to which the suit
could be applied, were admitted. Then the pressure
of a social environment in which contract was gradu-
ally supplanting custom caused a further relaxation,
and the inclusion of yet other classes of contracts,
by means of the *quid pro quo*, which, as we have

[1] 11 and 12 Edw. III. (Rolls), 587.

already seen, was closely connected, in the minds of
14th century judges, with the subject of proof. But
as this last doctrine was, in fact, infinitely more ex-
pansive than the archaic theory of *suit*, the latter died
away as its place was taken by its rival. The great
instance of suit, the parol sale, was, of course, amply
covered by the new doctrine. The cases of gratuitous
bailment were not; and it is not a little curious that
it was exactly the cases of gratuitous bailment which,
centuries later, proved so hard to reconcile with the
theory of consideration.

It now only remains for us to consider the part
played by Assumpsit in the development of the
doctrine.

One of the very latest, if not the latest, of the
instances of Assumpsit reported in the Year Books
is peculiarly important as bringing out the distinction
which existed between Debt and Assumpsit at the
end of our period. The plaintiff had imprisoned one
T. in the Counter for a debt, and the defendant went,
in the absence of the plaintiff, to the latter's wife,
and undertook to her (*assumpsit super se*) to pay the
debt if the plaintiff would discharge the prisoner.
The plaintiff subsequently returned home, and, being
informed of the circumstances by his wife, discharged
T., who failed to pay. Thereupon the plaintiff sued
the defendant in Case. At the trial, the defendant
relied on the inability of the wife to " be a party to
such an assumption," without the previous authority
of her husband. This objection was overruled, and
the defendant now moved in arrest of judgment,
alleging, amongst other exceptions, that the action

should have been Debt. But Brook, B., said—"I understand that one will not have the writ of Debt but where a contract is, for the defendant had not *quid pro quo*, but the action is solely founded on the assumption, which sounds merely in Covenant: and if it had been by specialty, the plaintiff would have had the action of Covenant, but being that he had no specialty, he had no remedy if not Action on his Case." Spelman and Port, J.J., although they agreed that the action was good, thought that the plaintiff might have brought Debt at his option, but the Chief Justice (Fitzjames) took Brook's view, saying—"for here is not any contract, nor did the defendant have *quid pro quo:* therefore he had no other remedy than Action on his Case. As if a stranger in London buy a piece of cloth, and I say to the merchant, 'if he does not pay you by such a day, I will pay:' *here is no contract* between the merchant and me, and he will not have the action of Debt against me[1]."

This is a very suggestive case, partly for the limits to the action of Debt alleged by the Chief Justice and Brook, and partly for the reasons alleged for allowing Case—that the plaintiff would otherwise have no remedy. It looks as though the older rule of *quid pro quo* (that the defendant must have some advantage) was being found too narrow in practice, but was too firmly seated to be openly displaced. The distinction, moreover, between the "contract" which will found the action of Debt, and the mere

---

[1] 27 Hen. VIII. 24 (3).

"agreement" which constitutes Assumption, is very curious.   The distinction had been taken in an older case, previously alluded to, where Prisot, J., said— "But in the case at bar he has not declared on a mere[1] contract, but only that an agreement was taken (*accord se prist*), on which it seems that this action (Debt) cannot be maintained[2]." It would, however, be wrong to lay much stress on the user of a technical term.   It seems likely that the expression "contract" came into English law through the writers who borrowed their language largely from Roman sources, and with them, of course, *contractus*, as distinguished from *pactum*, means an agreement upon which a normal action can be brought.   Thus the English legal vocabulary started with the word as a generic expression, which included specialties and even, probably, bailments.   In a case of Edward III., the reporter speaks of Debt as being demanded "part by obligation" (i. e. bond) "and part by *other* contract[3]."   A statute of Richard II. is equally comprehensive[4].   But in 22 Hen. VI.[5] we find the expression "simple contract" used repeatedly, though it may be, not precisely in its modern meaning; and in 39 Hen. VI. a member of the Court said that a party "should have brought his action on the specialty, *and not on the contract*[6]."   It looks, then, as if there were a tendency to separate "contract"

---

[1] ? "strict," "perfect."   [2] 37 Hen. VI. 8 (18).

[3] 42 Edw. III. 25 (10).   And see also 20 Hen. VI. 34 (4). ("In your case the contract is good without specialty.")

[4] 6 Ric. II. c. 2 (as to *Venue*).   [5] 22 Hen. VI. 36 (1).

[6] 39 Hen. VI. 34 (46).

from "specialty" on the one hand, and from mere "agreement" on the other.

Coming back to our first case of Assumpsit, we may, I think, take it for granted that the feeling which moved the Court to allow the plaintiff to succeed was the feeling that he had suffered damage by the defendant's conduct. This was a peculiarly appropriate ground in an action which was, at least technically, founded on tort; and the objection that the defendant received no benefit from the plaintiff's act (*quid pro quo*) would be immaterial. Hence we see how it was that the notion of the equivalent or, as we should say, *consideration*, would be different in the two instances of Debt and Assumpsit.

That the tortious character of the Action on the Case was recognized well into the 15th century is clear from many instances, some of which are exceedingly interesting. In the 12th year of Edward IV., a man brought the action against one to whom his (the plaintiff's) goods had been bailed by the plaintiff's bailee. One member of the Court (Brian, C. J.) thought that the plaintiff could not recover, *because the defendant was a stranger to the first bailment.* But he was overruled by all the other judges[1]. Again, the plaintiff succeeded in 20 Henry VI. in a bill of Deceit in the King's Bench, where we should now consider the matter purely one of contract. The complaint was that the defendant, after agreeing (*bargaina*) to sell land to the plaintiff, had enfeoffed another of it. The defendant objected that

---

[1] 12 Edw. IV. 13 (9).

the action should have been Covenant, but the Court overruled his objection, again chiefly on the ground that, as he had the action of Debt for his purchase money, it would be unjust to deprive the plaintiff of all remedy[1]. It should be noticed, however, that in a slightly earlier " Action on the Case in the nature of a writ of Deceit," where the plaintiff alleged that there was a " bargain " between him and the defendant, that he should marry the defendant's daughter, and that the defendant should enfeoff him of lands, and that the defendant had married his daughter to another, the plaintiff was defeated. One of the judges observed that "he has not declared that the defendant had *quid pro quo*, and so that cannot be called a bargain[2]." But this case, of course, brought in the debated point of jurisdiction, and moreover, it is easy to see that a very good defence might have been raised, on the ground that the marriage of the defendant's daughter to a third party was the act of the lady herself, not of the defendant. The actual ground of decision alleged is highly technical, and, moreover, not borne out by other cases[3].

We may now clear the ground by noticing at random a few of the instances in which Assumpsit was used, in the 15th century, as a remedy for breach of contract, marking specially anything which looks like a statement of consideration.

[1] 20 Hen. VI. 34 (4). The action had been allowed on similar acts in 16 Edw. IV. 9 (7).

[2] 7 Hen. VI. 1 (3).

[3] e.g. 16 Edw. IV. 9 (7). 14 Hen. VIII. 17 (6).

In a well known case of 2 Henry VII. the plaintiff sued for damages for the loss of his sheep which the defendant had to guard, and which "negligently by his default" were drowned. The Court was equally divided in opinion, principally on the ground that the allegation was one of nonfeasance. But Townsend, J., said—"When the party undertakes (*assume sur luy*) to guard the sheep, and afterwards allows them to perish by his default, seeing that he has taken upon himself to execute the bargain, and has them in his custody, and afterwards does not take care of them, the action lies[1]." In other words, Townsend thought it was not a mere non-feasance, if there had been a special undertaking, coupled with a bailment. Eighteen years later, a *dictum* of Fineux, C. J., goes still farther. "If I covenant for money to make a house by a certain day, and do not do it, Action on the Case lies for the non-feasance[2]." And in the next year the same learned judge observed—"If one covenants to build me a house by such a day, and he does nothing towards it, I have an Action on the Case for this non-feasance, just as well as if he had done it badly, *for I was in damage by it*[3]." It would be interesting to know if the Chief Justice meant to lay any stress on the pecuniary reward in the former case; for he makes no mention of it in the latter. By the term "covenant," he probably means only a verbal agreement, for if there were a specialty, there could be no

[1] 2 Hen. VII. 11 (9).   [2] 20 Hen. VII. 8 (18).
[3] 21 Hen. VII. 41 (66).

manner of doubt that the action of Covenant would be available.

In the year following the sheep decision, a man brought the Action on the Case, alleging that the defendant had undertaken *for a sum certain,* to wit £20, to labour on behalf of the plaintiff with *J.* for a lease to the plaintiff of the manor of Dale, and that he had induced *J.* to make the lease to himself. The Court held the defendant liable, on the ground that there had been a misfeasance[1].

Going back upwards of half a century, we get almost to the beginning of Assumpsit. In the 19th year of Henry VI. an action of Case was brought against R. Marshall, for that the defendant assumed to the plaintiff in London to cure his horse of a certain malady, and that he so negligently and improvidently applied medicines, that he killed the horse. The defendant pleaded that the assumption was made in Oxford and performed. The plaintiff demurred, alleging that the defendant ought to have traversed the negligence which was the gist of the action. But the Court was unanimous against him, saying that without the allegation of the assumpsit he could not succeed, unless he could prove that the defendant was a common marshal; and one judge said that the count of *negligenter apposuit* was void[2]. Five years before this, a man had brought Case, alleging a bargain for the purchase of land from the defendant for a certain sum, and a covenant by the

[1] 3 Hen. VII. 14 (20).

[2] 19 Hen. VI. 49 (5); see also *dictum* of Choke, 11 Ed. IV. 6 (10).

defendant to procure a release from strangers, which
release he had not procured[1]. There was a pure case
of non-feasance, but the writ was held good. Prior
to this decision there seems to be a considerable gap
in the history of Assumpsit. We may therefore, look
for a moment at the contemporary instances in which
the action was not allowed.

It appears that the liability of executors in Case
on a simple contract made by their testator was
doubtful. In a report of 12 Hen. VIII. it is stated
that the justices were unanimously of opinion that
the action lay, on two grounds; first, that the plaintiff
was without other remedy[2], and, second, *because the
plaintiff had acted upon the testator's promise*[3]. (It
was a case of guarantee for the purchase of goods.)
But the great authority of Fitzherbert, fourteen
years later, is strongly against the claim; that
learned judge denying *in toto* any liability on the
executors, and asserting that the decision in 12 Hen.
VIII. was bad law[4]. It should be observed, however,
that Fitzherbert's opinion is merely *obiter,* and that
in the earlier case the Chief Justice meets and turns
aside the maxim *actio moritur cum persona,* saying,
"for that is where the hurt or damage is corporal"
(for there the party cannot be punished after his
death)…"but in this case the plaintiff can have

[1] 14 Hen. VI. 18 (58).

[2] Debt would not lie, for two reasons; first because the contract
was verbal, admitting of wager of law, and, second, because there
was no advantage to the testator.

[3] 12 Hen. VIII. 11 (3).

[4] 27 Hen. VIII. 23 (21). "Mettez cest cas hors de vè Levres,
car il n'est Ley sans doubt."

what he would have had if the party had been alive, to wit, the price of his goods." But the reporter adds—"*Quære*, if the testator were alive, whether this action would lie against him, or he could wage his law in this case[1]."

Again, where a man brought Case on an ordinary contract for the purchase of malt, alleging what we should call a "conversion" by the defendant on his failure to deliver, the majority of the Court held that he should have claimed in Debt, "and where a general action lies, there the special action on the Case does not[2]."

And so where the claim was upon the bailment of a horse to safely guard *for a certain sum into the defendant's hands paid,* and the writ alleged that the defendant so negligently guarded the horse that for defect of care it died, the Court refused to allow the action. But it should be mentioned that in this instance the plaintiff had previously brought *Detinue,* and had been defeated in the wager of law[3].

What we may perhaps call the contractual limit of the action is clearly stated in a report of 21 Hen. VI. Taulbois brought Case against Sherman, counting that he had bargained with him at Lincoln for two pipes of wine for ten marks, and that the defendant ought to have delivered the wine at Golthall before a date then passed. One judge

---

[1] 12 Hen. VIII. 11 (3).

[2] 20 Hen. VII. 8 (18).

[3] 12 Edw. IV. 13 (10). Statham (*accion sur le Cas* 25) reports a similar decision in 27 Hen. VI. (Trinity), but I have not been able to trace the reference.

thought that the action should have been Debt, and another that it should have been Detinue, on the ground that by the bargain the property was in the plaintiff[1]. But the general opinion was that the failure to deliver could not be made the basis of Case. "For if a carpenter make a bargain or covenant with me to make a house sufficient and good, containing such a measurement, and by a certain day, if he makes me no house, I shall not have a writ of Trespass on the Case against him, but an action of Covenant, *if the covenant was written;* but if he makes the house contrary to my covenant, though my covenant was not written, I shall have against him the action of Trespass on the Case[2]."

It seems clear, then, that in 21 Hen. VI. the gist of the action was tort, not contract, and that tort implied positive act, not mere non-feasance. This view is, on the whole, borne out by the contemporary as well as the earlier cases, though there is evidently some difference of opinion among the judges. Thus in *Somerton's* case (reported three times under 11 Hen. VI.[3]) it was said that for non-feasance of an agreement made by "nude parol'" there was no remedy. Eight years earlier, in a very interesting action for not building a mill, the Court seemed undecided in the matter of the non-feasance, though the point was evaded[4]. But in 2 Hen. IV. (only a quarter of a century before the last case), assumpsit

[1] 21 Hen. VI. 55 (12).

[2] 21 Hen. VI. 55 (12).

[3] 11 Hen. VI. 18 (10), 24 (1), and 55 (26).

[4] 3 Hen. VI. 36 (33).

was brought against a carpenter for not building houses, the famous Gascoigne being the plaintiff's counsel[1]. The defendant urged that the matter was only Covenant, and the Court agreed. But Brenchesley, J., observed,—"Peradventure, if he had counted, or mentioned in the writ, that the thing had been commenced, and then by negligence nothing done, it would have been otherwise." And the same ruling was given nine years later[2].

But, of course, it was ultimately perceived that, for all practical purposes, a man might just as positively harm another by non-feasance as by misfeasance. As Babington said in the mill case— "Suppose a man makes a covenant with me to cover my hall or a certain house by a certain day, by which time he does not cover it, so that for defect of covering the timber of the house is all perished by the rain; in this case I say that I shall have good writ of Trespass on the matter shewn against him who made the covenant with me[3]." And this view received the support of *dicta* of high authority before the end of the period[4], though the old theory of misfeasance died hard[5].

We will now notice one or two cases which seem to bear upon our special subject of consideration, as connected with the action of Case. We remember that, quite at the end of our period, the King's

---

[1] 2 Hen. IV. 3 (9).

[2] 11 Hen. IV. 33 (60).   [3] 3 Hen. VI. 36 (33).

[4] 20 Hen. VII. 8 (18)—Frowike, C. J. 21 Hen. VII. 41 (66)—Fineux, C. J.

[5] e.g. 11 Edw. IV. 6 (10). Choke, on the surgeon.

Bench allowed the action to succeed on an Assumpsit, although the judges expressly pointed out that there was no *quid pro quo*[1]. This looks as though either *quid pro quo* was not consideration, or that consideration was not necessary in Assumpsit. But we must look at one or two other cases; and in them we shall notice that the plaintiff volunteers the statement of the recompense (e. g. *pro quadam pecunia* etc.), although the practice is by no means uniform. The reward was mentioned in the lease case in 3 Hen. VII.[2], in the case of the bailment of the horse in 12 Ed. IV.[3], in the case of the non-delivery of wine in 21 Hen. VI.[4], and in the case for not procuring the release in 14 Hen. VI[5]. But by far the most important reference to the matter is to be found in the mill case, in 3 Hen. VI[6].

Here the plaintiff brought trespass against Watkins of London, *mill-maker*, counting that the defendant took upon himself (*emprist sur luy*) to make a mill for the plaintiff, to be ready by a certain day, by which day the mill was not made. The defendant's counsel demanded judgment—"for by the writ it is supposed that the defendant should make a mill, and he has not declared it to be certain, what he should have for the making." Cokayne thought the objection immaterial, but Rolf said— "As to your first claim, it seems to me that he should have made express mention *in the writ* of what he ought to have had; and I say that there is

[1] 27 Hen. VIII. 24 (3).
[2] 3 Hen. VII. 14 (20).
[3] 12 Edw. IV. 13 (10).
[4] 21 Hen. VI. 55 (12).
[5] 14 Hen. VI. 18 (58).
[6] 3 Hen. VI. 36 (33).

a great difference between where one hires another
to make anything, and where there is a common
labourer; for the labourer can be put in certainty by
the Statute[1]; in which case though nothing was said
in the Covenant as to what he should have, the
servant will have a good action of Debt against him
for his wages according to the statute: but if I make
a covenant with one to go with me, or to make a
certain thing, and I do not put it in certainty what
he is to have for the making of the thing, in this case
I say that the covenant is void towards both parties;
for if he does not perform the covenant, I shall never
have an action against him, no more has he, if he
perform it, an action to demand anything for his
labour, unless it was made certain what he should
have : and so it seems to me that if this action on
this matter be maintained, that the principal thing
which *causes* the action must be openly declared in
the writ, and that is the covenant, which is not good
unless it be put in certainty what he should have."
Four years later it was expressly ruled that a man
who sues in Case must shew the special circumstances,
"comprising the substance of the matter," in the
writ, not merely in the count[2]. But, in Somerton's
case (11 Hen. VI.), an objection similar to that which
was allowed in the mill action was overruled by the
Court, Cotesmore saying[3]—"for it is supposed that
he was retained for a certain sum." These examples
seem to shew a reaction in favour of the principles

---

[1] i.e. the Statute of Labourers, which fixed the amount of
artisans' wages.

[2] 7 Hen. VI. 45 (24).   [3] 11 Hen. VI. 24 (1).

of Debt in the new action of Assumpsit. The latter
had been introduced, at least partly, to remedy the
anomaly of denying to a man who was liable to the
action of Debt on a certain transaction all remedy
against the other party for his default in the same
transaction. Therefore, if the other party could not
bring Debt, the reason for allowing Assumpsit failed.
And, as we have seen, the other party could only
bring Debt if his claim were for a sum certain.
Hence, apparently, arose the connection between
Assumpsit and recompense. Of course, it was
peculiarly appropriate that the Action on the
Case should be given to supply the defect of other
remedy, and the leaning in favour of the statement
of consideration shews that the action of Assumpsit
is rapidly losing its tortious character.

If, in conclusion, we trace back the action on the
Case to its earliest instances, we shall see how entirely innocent it is of all connection with consideration.
The intermediate step between the assumpsit-mis-
feasance cases of the early fifteenth century, and the
trespass cases of Edward III.'s reign appears to have
been the liability of the man who professed a
" common calling." In 39 Hen. VI. Moile, J., said—
" If I come to an innkeeper to lodge with him, and
he will not lodge me, I shall have an action of
trespass on the case against him[1]." And Paston, J.,
in the wine case, whilst agreeing with the actual
decision, expressed his opinion, that if a man ex-
ercising a common trade, such as a smith, refused a

[1] 39 Hen. VI. 18 (24).

reasonable request to work, accompanied by an offer of payment, and damage resulted from his refusal, he would be liable[1]. And in the case for negligently attending the horse, the same learned judge took the point that the defendant was not alleged to be "a common marshal[2]." In these cases of "common calling," proof of the assumption was unnecessary.

We now come to four cases of the reign of Edward III. which seem to shew us the action of Assumpsit in embryo. In 48 Edw. III. a man brought Case against a surgeon who had undertaken (*emprist*) to cure his hand which had been wounded, alleging that, by the negligence of the defendant and his cure, the hand was so impaired that the plaintiff suffered mayhem, to his wrong and damage. There was no mention of reward, and the reporter notes that the writ did not state the place *of the under-taking*, nor contain the words *vi et armis* or *contra pacem*. The defendant's counsel offered to wage his law as to the fact of agreement, but the plaintiff objected that this was a writ of Trespass, "and of a thing which lies in the cognizance of the jury (*pais*)," and that wager of law was not grantable. He was, however, overruled by the Court. Then the defendant objected that the place where the undertaking was made was not specified in the writ, by which default the Court could not know from what neighbourhood the jury should come. And this objection was ultimately allowed, and the writ abated; though the Court suggested as another reason that a remedy

---

[1] 19 Hen. VI. 49 (5).   [2] 21 Hen. VI. 55 (12).

by appeal of mayhem lay open to the plaintiff's wife, whereas in the case of a horse injured in shoeing, the horse could not have an action[1]! In other words, the undertaking was looked upon as an essential part of the case, and the action was really considered as one on contract, Cavendish, J., saying—"And also this action of Covenant by necessity is maintainable without specialty, because that for such a little thing a man cannot always have a clerk to make a specialty."

Two years earlier occurred the case which the Court distinguished from the last decision. There a man brought Trespass against a smith for laming his horse, and the writ ran—*quare clavem fixit in pede equi sui in certo loco per quod proficium equi sui per longum tempus amisit.* The defendant's counsel objected that this was a writ of Trespass, and that it did not contain the words *vi et armis.* But the Chief Justice (Finchden) said—"He has brought his writ on his case, so he frames his writ well." The defendant persisted that the allegation should have been either *vi et armis* or *maliciose fixit,* and also that, as there was no allegation of a bailment, the trespass, if any, must have been against the peace (because the horse would be in the plaintiff's possession). But the writ was agreed good, and the defendant was put to deny the laming[2]. In a similar case of 43 Edward III., the defendant objected that the plaintiff should have brought the writ of Trespass, "that he killed your horse generally." But Belknap, the plaintiff's counsel, denied this, saying that he

[1] 48 Edw. III. 6 (11).　　　[2] 46 Edw. III. 19 (19).

could not allege force; and the Court agreed with him. Then the defendant wanted to plead a denial of the undertaking. But the Court compelled him to deny the death of the horse through his default[1]. In these last two cases, it will be seen that the Court leaned strongly to the view that the tort was the real gist of the action.

The last report to notice in detail is the celebrated case in 22 Edw. III., in which *J.* complained by bill that *G.* on a certain day, at *B.* on Humber, had undertaken to carry his (*J's*) mare in his boat across the Humber safe and sound, but that the said *G.* there caused his boat to be overloaded with other horses, by which overloading the mare perished, to his tort and damage. *Richmond* (defendant's counsel). "Judgment on the bill, which alleges no tort in us, but proves that he would have an action *by writ* by way of Covenant or by way of Trespass." *Bank*[2]: "It seems that you did trespass when you overloaded the boat, by which his mare perished. Wherefore, answer[3]."

This case is usually quoted as an early instance of Assumpsit, but it is not quite clear that it bears out the view. It should be noticed that the defendant did not deny that the action was maintainable. He merely objected to the use of the special remedy by way of bill, when the ordinary remedy by writ was available. And the Court,

---

[1] 43 Edw. III. 33 (38). The writ ran—*manucepit equum prædicti Will' de infirmitate, et postea prædictus John ita negligenter curam suam fecit, quod equus suus interiit.*

[2] Does this mean " the Court," or Bankwell, J.?

[3] 22 Ass. 94 (41).

though overruling the technical objection, agreed with the view that the act complained of was a trespass, unless indeed the case (as is not unlikely) be wrongly reported. The editor's marginal note describes it as an "Action on the Case." But there is nothing in the report itself to shew any reference to the Statute of Westminster II. The matter is treated as one of ordinary trespass.

As it is proposed to conclude this essay with a summary of the whole history of the Doctrine of Consideration, it will hardly be necessary here to attempt to put the disjointed observations of this chapter into a connected form. We may notice, however, one or two points which obviously require a word of mention.

It will have been observed that our enquiry into the history of Consideration has proceeded without any help from Chancery sources, and, in face of the fact that text-book writers have assumed the Chancery origin of the whole doctrine[1], this course may have appeared unorthodox. But really there seems to be little evidence for the influence of Chancery[2]. It is true that the accessible Chancery records of the first three centuries are very meagre.

---

[1] e.g. Anson, p. 41.

[2] The only case directly bearing on the point which I can find is 37 Hen. VI. 13 (3), where the Chancellor made a man release a bond given for the purchase of debts, because it turned out that the debts could not be enforced, and so the plaintiff had not *quid pro quo*. But this was long after the doctrine of *quid pro quo* had been established in the Common Law Courts. The decision is, however, curious, as applying the doctrine to specialties.

But, had Chancery made a real point of the theory, we should surely have found some surviving maxim in which it was embodied, some fossil footprint in the plastic clay of Chancery doctrine. But where is such trace to be found? Equity acts *in personam*; equity "regards that as done which ought to be done"; and so forth. But never, "Equity aids a man who has given consideration." In fact, when Equity adopted contract law through the medium of Uses, she showed her dislike to the doctrine of Consideration by reducing it to its narrowest limits, by the admission of the "good" as distinguished from the "valuable" consideration.

On the other hand, there are facts which seem to point to the conclusion that the doctrine is quite innocent of Chancery origin. One is, that the action of Trespass on the Case, through which one very important part of it appeared, was an engine particularly encouraged by the Common Law Courts as a rival to Chancery. In a case in 21 Edward IV. Fairfax, J., said—"And so I counsel you to plead, and then the *Subpœna* would not be so often used as it is now, if we allowed such actions on the case, and maintained the jurisdiction of this Court and other Courts[1]." And in 21 Hen. VII., Fineux, C. J., in his dictum before quoted, re-marked—"And thus it is if one make a bargain with me, that I shall have his land to me and my heirs for £20, and that he will make the estate to

---

[1] 21 Edw. IV. 23 (6). It appears that Chancery used occasion-ally to entertain actions for non-feasance of a promise. (8 Edw. IV. 4 (11)).

me according to the covenant, I shall have action on my case, *and no need to sue a Subpœna*[1]." Nay, it was even suggested, in 21 Henry VIII., that a trustee could be made liable in Case as well as by Subpœna[2]."

Again, it may be well supposed that, if Chancery invented the doctrine of Consideration, some trace of it would be found in the other Courts formed under ecclesiastical influence. But we have seen that, in the elaborate discussion on the point in the *Doctor and Student*[3], the cleric is represented as entirely innocent of any acquaintance with it; in fact the whole of his argument turns on the view that it is the mental condition of the parties, and not the existence of consideration, which decides the validity of the contract. It is quite likely, though in the absence of evidence it is impossible to prove it, that the economic doctrine of consideration received some help from the "Law Merchant"; but one really fails to see that it would commend itself with any force to the minds of ecclesiastical school-men, who looked upon interest as unholy, and money as the root of all evil.

Finally, it may be asked—Is there anything to be gleaned from the name itself? It is said, by a

[1] 21 Hen. VII. 41 (66). It would now also be thought that the case in 3 Hen. VII. 14 (20), ante, p. 198, (where the defendant was employed to get a lease for the plaintiff, and got it for himself) was a matter for Chancery.

[2] 14 Hen. VIII. 24 (2). The application of the process of outlawry to the Action on the Case (by the 19 Hen. VII. c. 9), must have greatly increased its popularity.

[3] *Doctor and Student*, II. 24.

high authority[1], that the word "consideration" is not used before the reign of Elizabeth, and though this is not strictly correct, for it appears more than once in the second Dialogue of the *Doctor and Student*[2], first published in 1530, it is certain that the expression *quid pro quo* and other periphrases are the older forms. It is tempting, of course, to connect the term with the *consideratum est* of the judgment, of which Blackstone gives such a feeble explanation[3], and with the *conisaunz* of the early Year Books. But, in the absence of light upon our legal antiquities, such speculations are vain, and it is better to content ourselves with the scanty knowledge we have obtained.

---

[1] Holmes, *The Common Law*, p. 253.
[2] cap. 24, *passim*.　　　　　　[3] III. 396.

CHAPTER IV.

It is now time to abandon our crab-like method of procedure, and sum up, in historical order, the results of our investigation.

At some unknown point in the twelfth century, the royal officials began to manufacture, or at least to define, the English common law, by means of the *writ*, an instrument already familiar in other departments of royal administration. In theory merely an executive order, the writ original, issued by the King's Chancellor with the authority of the Great Seal, was in effect a statement of law. It was not, like its degenerate descendant, merely the formal initiative of legal process, but a declaration that if the person who applied for it could prove the facts which he alleged, he was entitled to relief.

In English, as in Roman law, the actions which first appeared in the state courts were actions to recover property and actions to obtain compensation for torts; the latter being, in most cases, actions founded on such torts as involved a breach of the royal peace. Thus appeared the various "Assizes" and the writ of Trespass. The only contractual action seems to have been that commenced by the writ of Covenant, to enforce the formal contract under seal, or at least (what would be an equally formal procedure in those days) in writing[1].

The actions to recover land seem long to have maintained their specific character, but at a very early date there appears to have been evolved a general action to recover chattels, the action of Debt. There can be little doubt that this was at first a real action, and that its gradual change towards a personal character was due to the increasing use of coined standard money, and the ultimate conviction that one set of coins was as good as another of the same economic value. To this change in the estimate of money, from a specific to a fungible article, we doubtless owe the marked tendency of the 12th and 13th centuries towards *adœratio*, or conversion of kind dues into money liabilities, as well as, incidentally, the change in the character of the action of Debt. The plaintiff no longer demanded of the defendant certain specific coins which he *detained;* he sued him for a certain sum which he *owed*. Of course, if the claim were not for money, but for non-fungible chattels, the old character of the action was, at least partially, continued; and so we get first the distinction between the *debet* and the *detinet,* and, ultimately, the severance of the action of *Detinue,* which the feudalists

[1] The distinction between the sealed document and the mere writing was taken as early as 30 Edw. I. (Rolls, 159).

would not call a real action, because it was not brought to recover a freehold, but which, nevertheless, was and remained a real action in idea.

Debt was by this time become a true action *in personam*, but an important trace of its original character survived in the rule that it could only be brought for a fixed sum—obviously because the old action of Debt had to be brought for specific chattels, coins or otherwise.

Our next hint comes from the subject of proof. Primitive tribunals know only formal methods of trial; consequently they recognize only formal methods of proof. In some cases proof and trial are the same thing; in others, trial is allowed as a kind of loophole of escape for the accused. The battle, the ordeal, and the compurgation are certainly of this character; and it is natural, therefore, that they should only be resorted to after a formal official proof, such as record, charter, or suit.

If our view of the latter institution be correct, the suit was originally composed of the official transaction-witnesses of the hundred and the burh, and could only be used to prove debts arising out of actual sales, loans, or bailments, effected in their presence. And as, of course, they were unlikely to be mistaken in such matters, their testimony could only be defeated by the severe test of the ordeal or the compurgation (the later " wager of law "). But the same reasoning would not apply in cases where their testimony would be merely to words or unimportant acts; and we cannot suppose that it was allowed to prove such facts until a method of trial more scientific than the ordeal and compurgation was invented.

But it so happened that, towards the end of the 12th century, such a method was invented, in the shape of trial by "Inquest" or "the country." And, almost immediately after the introduction of this method of trial, we find, as a matter of fact, that the suit is used for all manner of purposes, but merely now to raise a presumption which the inquest may disregard if it thinks fit.

Much, however, as the functions of the suit have expanded, and widely as it has departed from its original character, some traces of that character still cling to it. And, apparently, this trace especially, that as it was the original function of the suit to bear testimony to the transfer of property, so still the suit must testify to some advantage passed to the defendant, unless, indeed, the plaintiff has a formal proof, such as a tally. And so we get the rule, that for Debt there must be advantage received by the defendant, or *quid pro quo*, if there is no formal proof. And this in addition to the former rule, that the demand in Debt must be for a fixed sum. But these are and remain procedural rules only; they never become parts of substantive law. A man could never bring Debt unless he claimed a fixed sum and shewed *quid pro quo;* but it did not follow that he could not enforce his demand in another way.

By this process of development, the law of simple contract, hardly existing in Glanville's day, and scarcely needed by a society organized on the principle of *status*, began to make its appearance. But, as the status *régime* broke down in all directions, the need for a more comprehensive system of simple contract began to be very pressing. Such a need makes itself felt at similar stages in other societies, and the want is always supplied. But it is a matter of great importance how it is supplied.

Practically, there are two ways of meeting the difficulty. Legislators and judges may sanction the existence of certain particular contracts, such as hiring, exchange, agency, and so forth; and may refuse to enforce any arrangements which cannot be classed under one of the recognized heads. If this be the course adopted, we get an unscientific or merely empirical theory of contract, such as existed in Roman Law. Or, on the other hand, legislators and judges may enforce any agreements, provided they fulfil certain general conditions. In such an event we get a true scientific theory of contract. But it is extremely curious to note, that, as a rule, the scientific theory of contract comes in, not by the main and plain road of legislation, but by the sidepath of procedure.

This was emphatically the case in English law. The action of Debt had done its utmost when it enabled a man to recover on a contract by which his opponent had really received advantage, and in which the claim was for a definite sum. It made no provision for other cases.

But provision was ultimately made by what would seem, *à priori*, a most unlikely machinery.

We have said that the early writs original

practically made law. And the best proof of this assertion lies in the fact, that one of the first cares of the avowedly legislative body, the Parliament, after its appearance upon the scene, was to put a stop to the making of new writs by the Chancellor. This restriction, was, however, afterwards found to be too severe, and Parliament itself authorised the Chancellor, in the year 1285, to frame new writs in cases where the facts were analogous to those already recognized as good grounds of action.

Apparently, in acting upon this authority, the Chancellor took as his model the old Common Law writ of Trespass. Now the gist of the action of Trespass was that the plaintiff had been damaged by an act of the defendant which was also a breach of the peace. The new writ of "Trespass on the Case," as it was called, framed on the 24th chapter of the Statute of Westminster II., though it omitted the allegation *vi et armis*, retained the *contra pacem*, and asserted the damage to the plaintiff. It was, therefore, at first, a pure action on tort; and it lay in all cases in which the Chancellor thought that the plaintiff had suffered damage by the defendant's act; although the latter did not technically amount to breach of possession. In some respects the new action was inferior to the older remedies: for it did not permit of the process of outlawry being applied to a defendant who refused to appear—a privilege always belonging to Trespass proper, and granted to Debt by an early statute[1].

---

[1] 25 Edw. III. st. v. c. 17.

But the simplicity of its requirements and the width of its scope soon made it popular; and when it was ultimately put on the same footing in respect of outlawry as Trespass and Debt[1], it threatened to drive the latter out of existence.

Before it reached this point, however, the Action of Case had taken a very important development. As contractual engagements became more and more common, it became clear that one of the most effectual ways by which one man could damage another was by not fulfilling an undertaking upon which that other relied. At first, out of deference to the analogy of pure Trespass, the Courts declined to give relief unless the defendant had been guilty of a positive act of malfeasance or misfeasance. But the inconsistency of holding a man responsible for carrying out his undertaking badly, and letting him go scot free if he did not attempt to carry it out at all, ultimately became manifest; and non-feasance was admitted as a ground of Trespass on the Case. This view was also powerfully assisted by the reflection, that in many instances of simple contract (such as sale) one party was able, by virtue of the fact that he claimed a sum certain, to bring the action of Debt; while the other, unless he were allowed to bring Case, was without remedy for a breach of the very same contract. To primitive tribunals, such an anomaly would, doubtless, have seemed unimportant; or, rather, it would not have seemed an anomaly at all. But as modern notions

---

[1] By 19 Hen. VII. c. 9.

of reciprocity and justice began to prevail, the Courts became anxious to abrogate it by putting the parties on equal terms. And so, where a vendor could have brought Debt upon the failure of the purchaser to complete, the latter was allowed to bring Case, on a similar failure by the vendor.

Thus, briefly, it was that the enforceable parol contract, without which no modern society could exist for a day, made its appearance in English law. For if a man could get compensation for damage which accrued to him by breach of a parol undertaking, he could, practically, enforce a parol contract. And thus it was that the parol contract, when it did appear, appeared as the innominate "assumption," or undertaking, not as the sale, the hiring, or other specific arrangement. And so English law acquired a scientific theory of simple contract.

Of course the fact was at first distinguished under the cloak of tort. The undertaking, which was the real gist of the action, was treated as merely an incident, at most as a condition precedent to the defendant's liability. The contrast between Covenant and Assumpsit was carefully taken. But the truth could not long be concealed; and when Martin, J., in the mill case of 3 Henry VI.,[1] broke out with the objection that, if such an action were allowed, "a man would have trespass for the breach of any covenant in the world," he shewed a prophetic foresight which was none the less accurate that it was unwelcome. Under cover of an incident in tort,

[1] 3 Hen. VI. 36 (33).

the action on the simple contract had really made good its footing.

It may be asked—Were there *no* limits to the kind of undertaking which the Courts would thus indirectly enforce? Undoubtedly there were. The Court would give no damage for breach of an undertaking which contemplated an illegality, or a manifest impossibility, and so forth. But at first it would appear that there were no traces of Consideration or *quid pro quo*, in the Action on the Case.

To see how this requirement came in, we must again consider the question of evidence.

It seems quite clear that the old method of proof by *suit* was at one time or another used in the Action on the Case. The *et inde producit sectam* appears in the precedents of counts in Case given by Rastell, and, oddly enough, especially in the cases of assumpsit[1]. Doubtless, by Rastell's time, the offer had become a mere form; but, as historians know, such forms rarely exist unless they have once been realities. The puzzling question is—What could the suit have been called upon to prove in Assumpsit? And to this question we can give no positive answer. We can only suggest that the requirement of *quid pro quo*, which had become connected with the proof by suit in the action of Debt, carried over into the proof by suit in the action of Assumpsit; and that thus what had once been a mere rule of procedure became embodied as a principle in the incipient law of simple contract, and,

---

[1] Cf. Rastell, *Entries*, sub. tit. *Action sur le Case*.

being in fact an extremely elastic and sensible principle, commending itself to the appreciation of a society becoming every day more imbued with commercial ideas, it took firm root in English law about the end of the 15th century. Through the medium of *uses* it made its way into conveyancing, and, though it has never acquired in that domain the ascendancy which it has achieved in the realm of contract, it has been turned there to very useful purposes. The practical amalgamation of Debt and Assumpsit, which took place in the middle of the sixteenth century, did much to bring the theory of consideration to its present condition, especially by establishing the rule that detriment to the plaintiff was equally sufficient with benefit to the defendant. And from that time[1] we may perhaps reckon that the doctrine has become an essential part of the law of contract.

Subsequent developments have been matters of application and detail, rather than changes in principle. The doctrine of consideration, first evolved as a procedural rule of contract law, has been used as a test of *bona fides* as between rival claimants to property, as a condition the existence of which is essential to the validity of all simple contracts and of some specialty contracts, and as evidence of the intention of a purchaser as to the destination of the benefit of his purchase. On the other hand,

---

[1] The decision in *Greenleaf v. Barker* (Cro. Eliz. 194) was given in the year 1590; but Debt and Assumpsit had been practically rendered equivalents in 1557 (*Norwood v. Read*, Plowd. 180).

the legal view of the nature of consideration has been greatly liberalized, as the doctrine itself has passed from the region of procedure to the domain of substantive law. Any inconvenience suffered, any liability incurred, any trouble undertaken by the promisee, is sufficient to create consideration; likewise, any benefit, however problematical or apparently unimportant, received by the promisor at the instance or through the agency of the promisee. The Doctrine of Consideration has now become an essential part of English contract-law; one of the first things which a student of that law learns is, that Consideration is essential to the validity of every simple contract.

Nevertheless, forgotten as it may be, the procedural origin of the doctrine is responsible for more than one of its most striking features. Take, for example, the rule that the amount of the consideration given for a promise will not be enquired into by the Court. Had Consideration originally appeared as a substantive doctrine, we should probably have found that the amount of the recompense was a material point; for, without reasonable equivalent, a contract is, *pro tanto*, a gift. But, as consideration merely came in as a piece of evidence, the amount of it has always been regarded as immaterial to the *prima facie* validity of the contract, however important in supporting a charge of fraud. Hardly less striking, however, is the doctrine, so early laid down in *Nurse v. Barns*[1], that the amount of damages to be awarded for breach of a contract

---

[1] Sir Thos. Raymond, 77.

is in no way to be controlled by the amount of the consideration given—that it is the damage of the plaintiff, and not the advantage of the defendant, which is to be estimated—a doctrine which we probably owe to the tortious character of Assumpsit. To put it in modern language, a plaintiff is entitled —not to be placed in the position which he would have occupied if the contract had never been entered into—but, to be placed in the position which he would have occupied had the contract been fulfilled. It is the positive breach of contract, and not the mere failure to give a return for the consideration, which is the gist of the action.

On the whole, the great interest of the subject lies in the fact that it affords perhaps the best instance in the domain of legal biology of an unconscious adaptation of a rudimentary and apparently casual organ to important and complex purposes. Strange as it may appear to us, the notion of the reasonableness of a contract seems to be entirely foreign to the infancy of law. To primitive tribunals, the fact that a man gives value for a promise is no ground for enforcing that promise. The form in which the promise was made, the nature of the thing promised—these matters may be taken into account; but the return for the promise is immaterial. The doctrine of consideration was apparently unknown to the Roman jurists, the most famous and influential lawyers whom the world has ever seen[1]. It came into English law purely as a

[1] The only trace of it in Roman Law known to the writer is in the doctrine of *leonina societas*.

matter of accident, as an incidental consequence of a special manner of proof; and it was not until it was familiar in this capacity that men perceived its value as a doctrine of substantive law. Then indeed it was seen that in this mere procedural rule there lay the *desideratum* after which Roman law had so long blindly groped, a simple and easily recognizable test of the validity of a parol contract. The achievement had effected itself unconsciously, there was no need to struggle for its introduction. Moreover, it was an achievement which especially commended itself to the habits of thought which were rapidly impressing themselves upon the nation. The result may undoubtedly be claimed by the advocates of judicial legislation as one of the greatest proofs of the merit of judge-made law. It may also not unfairly be said to shew, at least in some degree, that the English nation, while it has perhaps produced few individual lawyers of genius, has in its corporate capacity manifested something like an unconscious genius for law.

For EU product safety concerns, contact us at Calle de José Abascal, 56–1°, 28003 Madrid, Spain or eugpsr@cambridge.org.

www.ingramcontent.com/pod-product-compliance
Ingram Content Group UK Ltd.
Pitfield, Milton Keynes, MK11 3LW, UK
UKHW012328130625
459647UK00009B/138